Why I am an Atheist
Who Believes in God

—

How to give love, create beauty and find peace

Frank Schaeffer

ISBN 13: 9781495955013
ISBN: 149595501X
Library of Congress Control Number: 2014903435
CreateSpace Independent Publishing Platform
North Charleston, South Carolina
PRINTED IN THE UNITED STATES OF AMERICA

Frank Schaeffer is a *New York Times* bestselling author of more than a dozen fiction and nonfiction books. Frank is a survivor of both polio and an evangelical/fundamentalist childhood, an acclaimed writer who overcame severe dyslexia, a home-schooled and self-taught documentary movie director, and a feature film director of four low-budget Hollywood features that Frank describes as "pretty terrible." He is also an artist with a loyal following of collectors who own many of his oil paintings. Frank's three semi-biographical novels (*Portofino, Zermatt* and *Saving Grandma)* describe growing up in a fundamentalist mission and have been translated into nine languages.

Follow Frank on Twitter www.twitter.com/frank_schaeffer
See Frank's paintings http://www.frankschaefferart.com/
Follow Frank on Facebook
https://www.facebook.com/frank.schaeffer.16
Contact Frank at http://www.frankschaeffer.com/

of religious fundamentalism, there is a beautiful place. There is room in this place for honesty. For tenderness. For fury. For wonder. For hope. For mistakes. For paradox. For grace. This book is written from that in-between place. It will help you get there too, if you're interested in finding it."—**Brian D. McLaren** author/speaker/activist

———

"A delight and charmer of a read—deft insights, burnished gold probes, arrow hit bull's-eye again and again." —**Ron Dart** (Thomas Merton Society of Canada)

———

PRAISE FOR FRANK SCHAEFFER'S OTHER BOOKS

THE GOD TRILOGY (*Crazy for God, Patience with God,* and *Sex, Mom and God*)
"A work that alternates from heartwarming to thought provoking to laugh out loud funny... Schaeffer brilliantly guides the reader through an exploration of the Bible's strange, intolerant, and sometimes frightening attitudes about sex..." — *Kirkus Reviews*

———

"Schaeffer's journey demonstrates that the world could be a better place if we were all able to reassess our beliefs and values-to examine them closely and glean only those worth saving." — *Library Journal*

———

"Frequently entertaining." — *The Humanist*

———

"To millions of evangelical Christians, the Schaeffer name is royal, and Frank is the reluctant, wayward, traitorous prince. His crime is not financial profligacy, like some pastors' sons, but turning his back on Christian conservatives." — *New York Times*

———

"Schaeffer is a good memoirist... As someone who has made redemption his work, he has, in fact, shown amazing grace." — **Jane Smiley in** *Washington Post*

———

"[Schaeffer's] readers—believers and non-believers alike—will be challenged to reconsider their views." — *The Daily Beast*

———

"[Schaeffer's] humor, at times of the laugh-out-loud variety, is abundant." — *San Francisco Book Review*

———

"Like Orwell [Schaeffer] became disillusioned with the extremism he encountered. Schaeffer fled the evangelical scene in the early 1990s... He now has created a thought-provoking analysis of the social and religious struggles that continue to define American consciousness." — *The Roanoke Times*

—

THE CALVIN BECKER TRILOGY of NOVELS (*Portofino,*
Zermatt **and** *Saving Grandma*)
"Poignant and hilarious Schaeffer is very funny, but we are never far from a sense that harshness and violence are real; we are never entirely sure how things will turn out." —**Richard Eder in**
Los Angeles Times

—

"The wonderful thing about this book is that like any really good vacation, it ends too soon." —*The Richmond Times-Dispatch*

—

"Beautifully written . . . great insight and unselfconscious humor." —*Publishers Weekly*

—

"A wry coming of age tale . . . splendid." —*Kirkus Reviews*

—

"A profound and sometimes painful look at the challenges of practicing faith, and a lot of fun to read." —*Washington Times*

———

"Told with warmth and humor." —*Library Journal* (**starred**)

———

"Mr. Schaeffer's gifts as a novelist are more than comic: *Saving Grandma* has a deeper river flowing through it as well, one that is sensual and loving and full of true grace. This is a wonderful book!" —**Andre Dubus III, author of** *House of Sand and Fog*

———

BABY JACK (a novel)
"The reader marvels at how Schaeffer makes this concise chorus of social conviction moving and memorable by emphasizing emotion over description." — *USA Today*

———

AND GOD SAID, "BILLY!"
"I love this novel… It's downright insightful throughout and takes readers deep into the shallow psyche of a sincere Charismatic-Evangelical whose God fails him. That failure turns out, through a

hilarious series of tragic-comic reversals, to be – let's just say something close to miraculous." — **Brian D. McLaren in *Huffington Post***

—

"… Honest, very funny and very serious. It's sure to rankle those who believe that being human means being certain." — **Kevin Miller director of *Hellbound? Patheos.com***

Books by Frank Schaeffer

Fiction

The Calvin Becker Trilogy of Novels:
PORTOFINO
ZERMATT
SAVING GRANDMA

———

BABY JACK
AND GOD SAID, "BILLY!"

———

Nonfiction

KEEPING FAITH—*A Father-Son Story about Love and the United States Marine Corps* (Coauthored with John Schaeffer)
FAITH OF OUR SONS—*A Father's Wartime Diary*
VOICES FROM THE FRONT—*Letters Home from America's Military Family*
AWOL—*The Unexcused Absence of America's Upper Classes from Military Service—and How It Hurts Our Country* (Coauthored with Kathy Roth-Douquet)
CRAZY FOR GOD—*How I Grew Up as One of the Elect, Helped Found the Religious Right, and Lived to Take All (or Almost All) of It Back*

Frank Schaeffer

PATIENCE WITH GOD—*Faith for People Who Don't Like Religion (or Atheism)*
SEX, MOM, AND GOD—*How the Bible's Strange Take on Sex Led to Crazy Politics—and How I Learned to Love Women (and Jesus) Anyway*
WHY I'M AN ATHEIST WHO BELIEVES IN GOD—*How to Create Beauty, Give Love and Find Peace*

for Genie

Contents

every moment
that pricked your heart
then broke it as it passed
will be gathered up

(From *One Day*—a poem by Katherine Venn*)*

I

I spilled my wine on a goddess and lived to tell the tale. Actually I splashed wine on a Swedish opera star, the lyric soprano Camilla Tilling. I was flying home to Boston from Mom's funeral. Camilla and I met because we were flying economy, and, I like to hope, because Mom wanted us to.

I can't afford business class but since Camilla is an opera star her contracts call for either first or business class travel. However, in Camilla's universe of priorities, being with her children and husband is more important than traveling in comfort. So Camilla asked her agent to spend the money she'd normally have used on swanky travel arrangements to bring her two young sons (ages four and two) and her husband along on many of her worldwide journeys to more than fifty concert and opera performances a year. Of course, when we met I knew none of this. That day she was traveling alone. And I learned about Camilla's life a bit later, after I spilled a plastic cup of red wine on her jeans.

Mom and I were both flying. We were on different airplanes but in the air at the same time. She was in a coffin and I was crammed into a narrow seat. Following a complex life, the start of Mom's afterlife was equally complex. That's why she was flying instead of resting in peace. Our family held the service in Switzerland in the small medieval stone church near where Mom died at age ninety-eight. Then Mom was shipped back to the States to be buried next to my father.

As I laid my hand on her coffin in farewell, I'd joked through tears to my daughter Jessica. "Noni finally figured a way to avoid security checks, *and* lie down the whole way!"

Jessica loved my mother passionately. She stood next to me, an accomplished forty-year old woman, holding me and weeping as we remembered how Mom had so often saved Jessica from me. I'd been a teen father, as ignorant of fatherhood as I was of life. Mom provided Jessica with love, an open door, and kindness without limits when I was clueless, impatient and mean.

The day before I met Camilla I'd been filling vases at the village fountain for the flowers I placed on either side of Mom's coffin. Two days later, I was feeling very alone as I boarded the plane. I was thinking about that fountain and all the times I'd hiked past it on walks with Dad. Now there was no longer any-one ahead of me to obscure the view of the cliff I was staggering toward one year at a time.

My flight from Zurich to Boston was overbooked. They bumped me from my aisle seat to a middle seat which put me next to a beautiful slim woman who reminded me of Jessica. Camilla got the aisle. Although offered money to fly the next day, she'd refused. Between my seat change and her near re-booking, the odds of meeting were rather slim.

Camilla had ash blond hair and a pale complexion. She looked as if she was in her twenties rather than twice that age and I knew she was Swedish. Jessica's daughter, my twenty-year-old granddaughter Amanda, speaks in a similar lilting Scandinavian sing-song voice, having grown up in the Swedish-speaking part of Finland. Like Amanda, Camilla was reserved and quiet— until she began to laugh. Her initial reserve hadn't put me off because it reminded me of many Scandinavians including my son-in-law Dani and my grandchildren Amanda and Ben (age seventeen) who seem quiet by American standards but are warm and outgoing in a frank and unassuming way.

When Camilla talked about her children and the music she loved, she flushed. The crimson splash of color moved from her neck to her cheeks like fire racing along the edge of a piece of paper. I described how my son John's children, Lucy age five, and Jack age three, come to my house every day, the central fact of my life we both understood as a mom and a grandfather. Then I knocked over my plastic cup of wine right after I learned Camilla sang on the great opera stages of the world in starring roles. The word *chagrined* barely describes my feelings. But Camilla said it was "nothing" and explained, "I'm a farmer's daughter from a small town in the middle of nowhere. I was so naive that when I got my first break I didn't even know who the conductor was. Don't worry about a little splash of wine."

In her fundamentalist teetotalling days before she loosened up and started drinking champagne in her eighties, Mom would have said that God planned my encounter with Camilla, notwithstanding our drinking wine together. Our meeting seemed to be part of what Mom called "God's plan for our lives."

I read about Camilla when I arrived home and the more I read the more it seemed to me that Mom had gleefully cooked up this entire adventure. Mom passionately loved classical music. She had pictures next to her bed showing her with various artists including Vladimir Horowitz. Mom had always defined herself by the music she loved and the concerts she'd taken her children to. Who else would have hung around the Steinway building in New York just for the fun of it every time she visited the city? Mom even wrote a book—*Forever Music* (1986)—about the way that music and the Steinway Company combined to somehow prove the existence of God!

Even the details of Camilla's recent performances seemed eerily meant to be. She had just sung the role of Angel in Handel's *La Resurrezione* at the Barbican in London. *La Resurrezione* was first performed in Rome on Easter Day 1708 and features a supernatural dialogue between Lucifer and an angel. I discovered Camilla is famous for singing the Angel role. The *Guardian* newspaper said, "Camilla Tilling's joyous Angel let fly volleys of flamboyant coloratura at Lorenzo Regazzo's Lucifer... while on Earth, John the Evangelist, Mary Magdalene and Mary Cleophas wait in tense anticipation for the dawn that will allow them to visit Christ's tomb and find it empty."

What were the odds of meeting someone on the way home from Edith Schaeffer's funeral of whom the *Times of London* enthused, "If you're choosing an Angel, you can't improve on the lightness and charm of the soprano Camilla Tilling." Camilla would have been Mom's perfect travel companion – an opera star who sings about Christ's empty tomb.

After we had talked about our lives, Camilla's music, my late mother and the many concerts she'd taken me to as a child, the conversation turned to God. As a young woman Camilla had sung in church and planned to become a primary school music teacher until, that is, she was discovered and rapidly promoted to leading roles in the Royal Opera Company and at Glyndebourne and around the world. So Camilla and I were both church kids! Camilla grew up in "a very religious household" while I grew up as the son of American evangelical missionaries who moved to Switzerland in 1947. In 1955 when I was three, they founded L'Abri Fellowship. As the years passed Mom and Dad went from obscurity to fame in Christian evangelical circles.

Mom would not have been so happy that Camilla and I compared notes on our spiritual journeys *out of* the evangelical religion we were raised in, but she would have loved our conversation about art, music, and the children who brought joy to our lives. The connections multiplied. We both grew up in small farming communities, one in Sweden and the other in Switzerland. Although no longer religious in the usual sense, Camilla said "Sometimes I have deep spiritual experiences when singing which give me hope that God exists." I told Camilla that I too am most spiritually inspired by music, art and my children and grandchildren. She spoke of the thrill of standing in the middle of an orchestra, hearing the "musicians breathe, to be so close to the heart of the music ..." Of her professional work, Camilla said, "I feel so much responsibility when I sing opera. Some people only go to one opera in their whole lives." I mentioned that my older grandchildren, Amanda and Ben, had grown up in her part of the world and told her how connected I feel to something bigger than myself when I paint. Then we talked about our vegetable gardens and also about what it's like to live in Switzerland as a foreigner—another experience we shared, though I had long since moved to America.

For many years Camilla had sung the role of Susanna in *The Marriage of Figaro* at the Royal Opera House in London's Covent Garden. We reviewed the redemptive story: Count Almaviva degenerates into a bullying, skirt-chasing baritone. Having given Figaro a job as head of his servant-staff, the count tries to obtain the favors of Figaro's bride-to-be, Susanna. So Figaro, Susanna, and the Countess conspire to embarrass the Count and expose his sexual scheming. The production shows the perils of uninhibited lust divorced from both good manners and honesty as well as the down side of unbridled hedonism. And above all it is Mozart's glorious statement about grace and forgiveness. We both noted that discussing this opera and its meaning was just another example of how the art we both loved inescapably plunged us back time and again into the realm of our spiritual pasts and journeys, no matter what we said we believed or did not believe on any given day.

We parted after I wrote out some hotel and travel information for the area of Italy where I'd set my novel *Portofino*. Camilla was looking for a place her children would enjoy vacationing, "where I can travel by train from Switzerland, because we do too much flying. I want to discover a place we can return to each year so it becomes familiar to my children. I'd like them to learn some Italian the way you did as a child."

I was thrilled that Camilla was so pleased to learn about the little beach that occupied a golden place in my happiest childhood memories. Mom was the reason I'd gone to Portofino from the time I was five until I grew up. So the flight ended in the rosy glow of vivid memories of my young, beautiful mother as she swam in her beloved Mediterranean Sea. Dreamlike as this encounter was, as we left the aircraft, the blotch of wine I saw on her jeans proved that Camilla had actually sat next to me.

A few months after meeting Camilla I watched my five-year-old granddaughter Lucy and my three-year-old grandson Jack sitting in silence on my bedroom floor, slowly turning the pages of a book written and illustrated by my friend Holly Meade. A cosmic eye blink ago they had been swimming in amniotic fluid, as if reenacting our 3.6-billion-year evolutionary journey from single cells to humans. Yet after what seemed like a second or two from their births, my grandchildren were riveted by the power of art. Something mysterious was happening: two little primate members of one of the oldest surviving placental mammal groups were having an aesthetic experience beyond mere survival.

Although I love Lucy and Jack for biological reasons—the imperative to pass on my genes— I found myself experiencing a profound upwelling of bliss. I understand why I'd feed and clothe my grandchildren, even love and cuddle them. But art?

My brain is not evolved enough to reconcile the collision of my genetic imperative with transcendent experience. My brain recognizes but can't explain how love and beauty intersect with the prime directive of evolution: *survive.* Nor can I reconcile these ideas: "I know that the only thing that exists is this material universe," and "I know that my redeemer liveth." Depending on the day you ask me, both statements seem true. So do these two statements seem true: "Mom sent me Camilla," and "Mom is dead and so can't send anyone anywhere." They both seem true though I have no idea what the word *true* means.

———

Mom died in March of 2013. Genie's and my friend Holly Meade died in June. It was a season of endings demanding reflection. Holly lived just long enough to meet her first grandchild and love him passionately during her final cancer-shadowed year before she was gone. Her last burst of creative fire, buoyant and infused with a spiritual lightness of being, made her passing seem all the more tragic to us, though not to her. Holly confronted her looming death with more grace than anyone I've ever known.

The first time I saw Holly was at a party. She seemed to materialize magically with the words, "Are you Frank Schaeffer? I read your novel *Portofino* and loved it. You made me laugh." The woman complimenting me had thick, long, wavy, sandy-blond hair tied back loosely with a silver clasp, large bright gray eyes, high cheekbones, finely wrought features, and flawless, pale skin. This person radiating intelligence, strength and serious purpose had just sought me out to compliment my writing! How often does *that* happen?

We sipped champagne and talked about Holly's art, my writing and our mutually abandoned evangelical beliefs, which had left us both deeply conflicted and yet still longing for something more than the here and now. A few days later Genie met Holly and we all became friends.

Holly's work had always been joyful. She covered sheets of paper with washes of watercolor and arranged cut shapes to produce pictures of startling clarity for her book illustration collages. Her woodcuts included angels with paper doll wings wearing party noses. She made funny prints, too, like the one entitled "We Have a Situation Here" featuring a pilot glancing out the cockpit window at a woman sitting on a flying carpet. Her lyrical print, "Love Up to Here," depicted a sensuous red and yellow female figure floating in midair enveloped in swirling mist.

Holly met Lucy just once, though when Lucy was with me they chatted whenever Holly called. (Jack was too young to remember Holly, and my older grandchildren, Amanda and Ben, live in Europe, as I said, and had never met Holly. I kept her posted about all their lives.) Lucy received wonderful packages full of Holly's big, glossy picture books. They arrived with elaborate address labels decorated with Holly's drawings. I told Holly about reading with Lucy and which books were her favorites. Holly became an almost mythical being to Lucy. "Holly Meade"—Lucy always called Holly by her full name as if referring to a royal personage—was the magical provider of favorite books *and* the bestower of a framed piece of original artwork. It hangs above her bed. When Holly died, Lucy exclaimed, "I won't have any more new Holly Meade books to read!" and she wept.

When Holly lived nearby in Newburyport, Massachusetts, my wife Genie and I saw her often. Due to soaring real estate taxes she sold her house and moved north to, as she put it, "live within my means." She wanted to do more "serious play"—creating and printing her woodcuts—and less book illustration work that provided her income. Holly reorganized her life in favor of art, living four hours away from us in Sedgwick, Maine.

The last shreds of my illusion of immortality were cremated along with Holly. Her death broke through my innermost protective layer of denial that had survived Mom's and, years before, Dad's passing. Until Holly's death, a residual echo of my comforting childhood faith about ultimate purpose and eternal life had softened the blow of the losses I found myself lamenting.

II

Whatever the source of art and religion, I was *personally* conditioned by my evangelical missionary parents to believe that I hear the voice of my Creator. This was no more a choice than my guilt feelings are. My mother and father believed in love as a spiritual reality and taught me to equate failure to love with sin. They believed that to be kind is to be in tune with the way things *are,* or to be in tune with the way things *would have been* if there had been no fall from grace in the Garden of Eden. My evangelical parents were not stupid, so either they didn't really believe Eden existed, or some part of their otherwise intelligent brains snapped when they adopted the one-size-fits-all born-again version of American fundamentalist Christianity.

Maybe the point is not what did or did not *happen*, but what is always *happening*.

Just because there was no Eden doesn't mean there never will be one. I experience Eden all the time. For instance, Lucy gazes at Botticelli's pictures and says, "Let's play Simonetta Vespucci!" Simonetta was Botticelli's model for at least one figure in the *Primavera*. After she died Botticelli painted her from memory again and again, finally asking to be buried at her feet.

Lucy climbs onto a chair and poses while I play Botticelli and draw her. Then we swap places and Lucy plays Botticelli and draws me. Because Botticelli loved, painted and mourned his Simonetta before she died at twenty-three, her meaning survives. Because Lucy is loved and has a winsome imagination she becomes my Eden. I also experience the fall from grace. Sometimes I shout at Lucy and Jack and they cry. I cast myself out of the garden.

Ironically, although Mom and Dad may have been deluded by their fundamentalist certainties, I am mostly at peace in my home where Lucy, Jack and I play Botticelli *because* I was indoctrinated with knee-jerk guilt. I realize now that my parents were often right for the wrong reasons. For instance, I feel guilt when I shout at Lucy and Jack. And when it comes to the "big sins" I would not have burned in hell for sleeping with the many women I've looked at longingly, but adultery would have ruined my marriage and the home where I play with my grandchildren.

My bias against adultery was instilled as a child hearing the command "Thou shalt not commit adultery," derived from a tribal myth about God proclaiming the law from a mountaintop. Myth or not, I sometimes like the result of my parents' delusions. Since my marriage has led to a personal Eden—punctuated by self-made hell from time to time—it is worth defending against my primate impulse to lash out at children, let alone to have sex with every fertile female I encounter.

Sometimes irrational guilt is all that's stood between me and terminal regret. As a teen father I slapped my daughter. These days I shout at my grandchildren once in a long while. There are more Edens within reach because I've listened to my guilt, not just made excuses. Sometimes irrational guilt is all I've had standing between me and regret.

Maybe from time to time irrational guilt is truer than mere fact. Maybe saying "evolution teaches" or "God says" is more or less the same thing: just another way of summing up what we know about ourselves from our collective human primate experience of what works.

⎯⎯⎯

Speaking of paradises lost, if there never was an ideal state of consciousness with which to compare my shortcomings, then why do I feel so bad when I scream at Genie? My faith that someday I'll be kinder to Genie, just as I'm kinder now than I was at eighteen, sustains my hope that things will get better. So does the fact I'm a far better grandfather than I was a father.

Acceding to researchers in the field of epigenetics, traumatic experiences produce fearful memories that are passed to future generations. A study carried out on mice in 2013 found that they could produce offspring with an aversion to actions and events associated with their parents' negative experiences. Nature and nurture turn out to be interrelated. Not only do our experiences change our genes but they also change our children's genes. So I'm glad I am nicer to my grandchildren than I was to my children. I'm glad I haven't entirely escaped the emotional alternative religious reality in which I was raised. Guilt is underrated.

Saying "I'm sorry" repairs the relationships I care about most. It's why my world is still intact. It's why there has been enough continuity and forgiveness leavening my life so that my son John and his wife Becky have stayed nearby and honor Genie and me with the joy of hands-on grandparenting. My guilt-inducing conscience is the bedrock of the grownup friendships Genie and I share with our children. Our relationship is founded on me saying "I am so very sorry for being an asshole" and then working to change. What I fear today isn't God's theoretical wrath but my family's palpable sorrow when I hurt them. That is hell in the here and now, the only hell there is. I can choose not to pass that hell on, as the epigenetic scientists confirm.

———

My kaleidoscopic beliefs are fickle and motivated by desire, wishful thinking, and wanting to fit in with my family and community and to make my marriage work. My dogmatic declarations of faith once provided status, ego-stroking power over others and a much better income than I've ever earned since fleeing the evangelical machine. Certainty made things simple, gave me an answer to every question *and* paid the bills.

With the acceptance of paradox came a new and blessed *uncertainty* that began to heal the mental illness called certainty, the kind of certainty that told me that my job was to be head of the home and to order around my wife and children because "the Bible says so." Embracing paradox helped me discover that religion is a neurological disorder for which faith is the only cure.

———

These days I hold two ideas about God *simultaneously*: he, she or it *exists* and he she or it *doesn't exist*. I don't seesaw between these opposites; I embrace them. I don't view this embrace as requiring a choice between mere emotion and fact, or between evolutionary biology and spirituality. Reality can't be so neatly parsed. Neuroscientists who analyze our chemistry-based brains still fall in love. Preachers declaiming a literal view of the Bible and a so-called young earth still use petroleum products only found because geologists operate on the premise that the earth is 4.54 billion years old.

I don't view my embrace of opposites as a kind of agnosticism. I view it as the way things actually *are*. An agnostic neither believes nor disbelieves in God. I'm not that person. I believe *and* don't believe at the same time. Gary Gutting made this point—or rather he provided a forum for someone else to make the point.

Gutting is a philosophy professor at the University of Notre Dame. He interviewed Howard Wettstein, a professor of philosophy at the University of California. The result was published in the *New York Times* (March 31, 2014) as "Is Belief a Jewish Notion?" Given what I'm writing here Gutting might as well have been addressing his questions to me. And Wettstein's answers are what I would have liked to have said had I been asked this question:

> **Gutting:** You say you're a naturalist and deny that there are any supernatural beings, yet you're a practicing Jew and deny that you're an atheist. What's going on here?
>
> **Wettstein:** Let's begin with a distinction between participation in a practice and the activity of theorizing, philosophically and otherwise … My thought is that 'existence' is, pro or con, the wrong idea for God. My relation to God has come to be a pillar of my life, in prayer, in experience of the wonders and the awfulness of our world … To see God as existing in such a domain is to speak as if he had substance … as if he were composed of the stuff of spirit, as are, perhaps, human souls. Such talk is unintelligible to me. I don't get it. The *theism-atheism-agnosticism* trio presumes that the real question is whether God exists. I'm suggesting that the real question is otherwise and that I don't see my outlook in terms of that trio … The

real question is one's relation to God, the role God plays in one's life, the character of one's spiritual life. Let me explain. Religious life, at least as it is for me, does not involve anything like a well-defined concept of God, a concept of the kind that a philosopher could live with. What is fundamental is the experience of God, for example in prayer or in life's stunning moments. Prayer, when it works, yields an awe-infused sense of having made contact, or almost having done so. Having made contact that is, concerning the things that matter most …These experiences are not theory-driven. The perceptions and understandings of the religious practitioner are more like the outpourings of a poet than they are like theoretical pronouncements… Poetry, at its most profound, need not observe consistency…

⸺

Maybe we need a new category other than *theism, atheism* or *agnosticism* that takes paradox and unknowing into account. I believe that life evolved by natural selection. I believe that evolutionary psychology explains away altruism and debunks love and that brain chemistry undermines my illusion of free will and personhood. I *also* believe that the spiritual reality hovering over, in and through me calls me to love, trust and hear the voice of my Creator. It seems to me that there is an off-stage and an on-stage quality to my existence. I live on-stage, but I sense another crew working off stage. Sometimes I hear their voices singing in a way that's as eerily beautiful as the off-stage chorus in an opera.

III

My youngest grandchildren Lucy and Jack are still comfortable with a paradoxical way of seeing reality. For them make-believe and the material universe merge in a poetic non-literal way that mirrors the scientific finding that one particle can instantaneously affect another particle light-years away or even be in two places at once. Schrödinger, the Austrian physicist who developed the field of quantum theory, called this idea "entanglement." Einstein called it "spooky action at a distance." Lucy and Jack just accept that life is weird, wonderful and defined by imagination.

Lucy and Jack seem to accept that something may never have happened but can still be true. They take Bible stories we read at face value and yet I see a flicker in their eyes that tells me that they already know the stories are not true in the same way boiling water is true and can be tested—it's hot!

When they're older, maybe my grandchildren will embrace apophatic theology, the theology of not knowing. Maybe they will look for ways to make the irrational rational by hiding behind words like "mystery" in order to sustain their faith. Apophatic theology teaches that the divine is ineffable and recognized only when it's felt. In contrast to the literalistic evangelicals and Roman Catholics, Eastern Orthodox, Muslims and

Orthodox Jews, some of the earliest Church Fathers were closer in their thinking to Wettstein. They said that scripture was to be read through an apophatic approach. Tertullian said, "That which is infinite is known only to itself." St. Cyril of Jerusalem said, "For we may not explain what God is but candidly confess that we have not exact knowledge concerning Him." In other words, the word *God* was to be understood by *not* understanding it.

The words *objective reality* are just a metaphor for something I'll never encounter. Lucy's and Jack's universe is more dependable and predictable than mine. They still think that what they observe is what is there. Their world is a safe place where parents stay married and there's no need to justify clinging to a sustaining myth by embracing fancy terms like *apophatic* or *mystery*. My son John and his wife Becky come home after work each day and routines are kept. Ba (that's me) and Nana (that's Genie) are always "at Ba and Nana's house." And Jack and Lucy still believe that Genie and I can answer their questions, even guarantee the future.

At the ripe old age of five, Lucy was pondering death. She asked why my mother had died and I told her it was because "Mom was very old." Then Holly died. A few weeks later as we walked up the drive, Lucy took my hand and quietly said, "Ba, when you pray in the morning, please ask God to make you grow old slowly."

"Okay, I will," I said.

A few days later we were walking up the drive again and I said, "How long do you want me to live?"

Lucy thought about it for a long moment and then answered, "I want you to live until my children are… twelve years old."

"Okay, I'll try," I said.

Of course, I have no idea what the right age is to die, just as Lucy thinks that twelve is old. She also told me, "The sun is really big, even though it looks small." I asked her how big, and she said, "It's *really* big, as big as a tree!"

Lucy's sense of time, place and scale is no more or less misinformed than mine. The only things in life I have fairly complete information about are minor household appliances. As for when to die, what to believe, whom to marry, where to live, whether or not God exists, when to have children, and what work to do, I think all this big stuff—stuff as "big as a tree!"—is best left to chance. My illusion of control over my life is long gone. I am *part* of a story; I am not *the* story. I've given up on planning. Rather, I plan while hoping that my plans won't work. I've experienced the serendipity of my plans failing. Then my failures sometimes open doors to things better than those I'd wished for. I was pissed off with the Swiss national airline for bumping me to a center seat. Then I met Camilla.

Anyway, since no one is ever just one thing, who are we planning *for*? Which "me" should be running the show? We're all in the closet, so to speak. We barely come out to ourselves and never completely to others. I've never met an unequivocal atheist or religious believer. I've only met people of two, three or four or more minds—people just like me. Atheists sometimes pray and eloquent preachers secretly harbor doubts. The evangelist Billy Graham preached certain salvation and heaven guaranteed yet privately told my dad, a friend and fellow evangelist, that he feared death and had many doubts.

We're all of at least two minds. We play a role and define that role as "me" because labels and membership in a tribe make the world feel a little safer. When I was raising my children, I pretended to be grown-up Daddy. But alone with my thoughts, I was still just me. I'm older now, and some younger people may think I know something. I do! I know how much I can never know.

Muslim, Jew, Hindu or Christian, you are that because of where and when you were born. If you are an atheist, you are that because of a book or two you read, or who your parents were and the century in which you were born. Don't delude yourself: there are no good reasons for anything, just circumstances.

Don't delude yourself: you may describe yourself to others by claiming a label of *atheist, Jew, evangelical, gay* or *straight* but you know that you are really lots more complicated than that, a gene-driven primate *and* something *more*. Want to be sure you have THE TRUTH about yourself and want to be consistent to that truth? Then prepare to go mad. Or prepare to turn off your brain and cling to some form or other of fundamentalism, be that religious or secular.

You will always be more than one person. You will always embody contradiction. You—like some sort of quantum mechanicals physics experiment—will always be in two places at once.

———

Lamby emphatically must *not* be in two places at once! Lamby is not quantum, apophatic or mysterious! Lamby is not a metaphor. Lamby is real.

Lamby became a pale, gray, tattered, ghost-lamb-guardian-angel long ago a falling apart shadow of her former stuffed animal self that graced Lucy's crib. Lamby—*the* Lamby—has been clutched nearly to death. She's been dragged along to doctor's appointments. She's been vomited upon and has soaked up many a hot tear from Lucy's face. Since Lucy can't get to sleep without Lamby, John and Becky know that Lamby must never be lost, washed or changed in any way that defiles her identity or even alters her familiar musty scent. Above all, she must survive—forever! So Lamby is delivered periodically to Genie's sewing room, where Lamby is resurrected.

Genie is the goddess who makes Lamby grow old slowly. Someday Lucy will say goodbye to her Lamby. For now, Genie answers her prayers. I hope God is as dependable, as real, and half as nice as Genie. This hope may be the only real indication that perhaps God exists. Be that as it may, God is my Lamby even when I don't believe in him, her or it. And if I change my mind someday, choose to think in black and white categories and become a single-minded atheist, I'll bet the first thing I'll do is ask God to help me to forget him, her or it. Then I'll cry myself to sleep, because I need my Lamby. In other words I am inconsistent and vulnerable.

IV

Genie and I drove to Sedgwick to visit Holly the week before she entered the hospital for the last time. We didn't know it was our final visit. Surrounded by her art, her two cats and her books, Holly looked vibrantly alive. Her hair had grown back from the last chemotherapy protocol. The short-cropped look suited her, although her sandy blond hair had turned Arctic fox silver.

Holly held my hand while she described her plans for the art gallery she'd recently added to her home. Her grip was vise-strong from years of cutting woodblocks and printing by hand. When we said goodbye, Holly, Genie and I clung to each other. But our last embrace didn't feel like a final farewell. I thought that she had more time.

A few days later we were shocked to hear Holly had died. Holly would not have shared my view of her death as tragic. She would resent her experience of illness being described as sad, though she suffered horribly. Holly was uncompromisingly hopeful.

Holly had declared that she was done "with more chemo craziness" and wanted to die "with my eyebrows on." So Genie and I were relieved that she died without another round of treatments.

In his eulogy, Holly's son Noah said, "My mother's creed was 'create beauty, give love, find peace.'" That's the best description of the *point* of living I've ever heard. In fact my mother proved that point with her life, too. After Mom died, I received hundreds of notes from people who read my tribute to her, the basis of a top-of-the-page-big-picture-included-world-leader-dies *New York Times* obituary. Mom would have been thrilled. The *Times'* book section editors ignored her many books, never reviewing any of them. So Mom would have loved that she finally made it into the "paper of record." It might have been worth dying for!

The notes, emails and texts I received included an email from a hotel maid Mom had talked to over forty years before when my mother found her crying in a hallway. Mom stopped to help, changed her schedule, missed an important book event at a big bookstore in downtown Manhattan and then invited this stranger to visit us. Another note came from a successful woman who had once been a pregnant teen whom Mom took into our home. A jilted wife, contemplating suicide until Mom gave her new hope, wrote that Mom saved her life. And there was a text message from an African-American couple my mother had sent money to almost fifty years before when she learned they couldn't pay their bills, and so on and on and on...

Mom would have said she did these things because she was following Jesus. She thought that to follow Jesus meant declaring that every word of the Bible is literally true. My mother affirmed this belief again and again, as if endless repetition that "the Bible is without error" would make it so. Her belief in a perfect Bible was a paradox, because Mom knew that the Bible was written by men. She knew that no men are perfect, not even her famous preacher husband, who hit her from time to time.

Luckily for the people she helped, my mother was gloriously inconsistent. She lived according to the more enlightened parts of the Bible and ignored the rest. For instance, no matter what she *claimed* the Bible taught about homosexuality, Mom *acted* as if being born gay was just another way to be human. She provided refuge, love and compassion to many gay men and lesbians at L'Abri, long before the secular world began to acknowledge that gay people are normal and healthy.

Dad and Mom had a lesbian couple living in our chalet for several years in the early 1970s. One was Dad's secretary, the other Mom's helper. They shared a room. Fortunately, my parents were hypocritical and acted as if, no matter their official religious absolutes, the higher call was to ignore what the Bible *said* in favor of what they hoped it *meant.* Thus, without ever saying it, it seems to me my parents were affirming that the Bible should be read as if Jesus was the only lens through which to see God. The result was that Francis and Edith Schaeffer were nicer than their official theology.

I never say "I'm sorry" to Genie without remembering who showed me how words of repentance backed up with action can change reality. Mom proved by her actions that an individual can behave *as if* another million years or so of ethical evolution has already happened. She'd stumbled onto a Jesus-motivated shortcut to a higher state of moral consciousness. She's taken charge of her own ethical evolution.

My parents stayed married because my father tearfully apologized for hitting Mom and then worked to curb his violent dominant male temper. The redemptive message or fairytales in which Mom and Dad believed were their path to a life infused with hope and light. Their theological certainties, delusional or otherwise, motivated them to provide many people with meaningful real-life encounters with goodness and mercy.

So who is actually delusional? Who is actually following Jesus: fundamentalist Christians rejecting gay men and lesbians' right to marry, or atheist humanists treating men and women with love and dignity? Fact-based, enlightened atheists sometimes treat people like shit, and delusional fundamentalists sometimes miss a book event in order to help a lonely hotel maid. Labels don't mean anything. Who cares about labels when someone is slapping you in the face? Who cares about labels when someone is saving you from drowning?

Who someone is and what they *do* is all that matters. This is especially true because who we are changes as we grow and as we change our minds. Furthermore, we are never really of one mind about anything. Belief is never the point—actions are. We can be of two minds about biology or God but treat everyone around us with kindness.

If we wait for correct ideas to save us—theological or otherwise—we'll never be saved, even from ourselves. Why? Because we can never have a fully correct idea. Why? Because however we label ourselves, we are still only half-evolved primates in two or more minds and multiple moods.

All we have is our stories. Today's great art is tomorrow's joke. Today's joke is tomorrow's great art. Today's atheist is tomorrow's ardent convert. Today's preacher is tomorrow's atheist author. I can't objectively describe reality because I'm trapped in the moving target we call time. That's what the word "evolution" means. The very fabric of the universe is unknowable and stranger than we can imagine and has a message for us: climb down off that high atheist, religious or agnostic pedestal!

V

Let's imagine I happen to be writing some sort of truth here. By the time you read this, I might have changed my mind. Ten years from now, I would likely put it differently. By then I may regret that I wrote this. And regardless of how I feel then, I'll bet that if you reread my book twenty years from now, you'll have changed, so the book will have changed, too. So much for changeless truth.

The brain has evolved to do one thing: process our environment and give us an illusion of certainty. We are programmed by our genetic prime directive—*survive*. This does not equip us to be all-knowing theologians, much less philosophers. We bestow meaning rather than discover it. We call an artist's mistress posing for a portrait a Madonna, and from then on any young woman with a baby and a halo is "the Madonna." Our brains have evolved to seek patterns. We test those patterns and discover useful ways of perceiving what's around us. Our perception is not reality.

We create a narrative. We want to see where we fit. Humans latch on to one-size-fits-all frameworks and use our catch-all truths that we label as science, Hinduism, Christianity or whatever, to explain everything. Evolutionary psychologists, biologists, philosophers, atheists, religious fundamentalists, liberals and conservatives, writers, hotel maids and preachers, we all act as if our pet paradigm can be stretched to fit every case. A little subjective pattern making by whatever name is stretched to make vast cosmological, artistic or philosophical projections, including this one. In fact our psychological needs, backgrounds, wounds and pain are the real source of our so-called beliefs and why we hang on to them or reject them. In that sense the most intellectual career paths are the most delusional. When it comes to drawing meaningful conclusions what use is an earnest five, ten or even twenty-year course of study as seen in the context of a multi-billion-year-old universe?

There are no objective facts, just personal histories and the coincidences of time and place seen through the lenses of short lives. Deal with it.

When we try to extend our narrative into unrelated areas— theology into biology or science into art—we create stories that explain everything and mean nothing. As Howard Wettstein says in the Gary Gutting *Times* interview:

> As religiously powerful as it is, the anthropomorphized sense of the divine coexists with the humble sense that we are over our heads. This latter feeling can itself be infused with awe. It can have its own religious power ... One of my complaints about the New Atheists, like Richard Dawkins, is their reductive tendency. I don't see why the psychological (or more generally naturalistic scientific) explicability of a phenomenon should suggest that questions associated with its meaning are put to rest. Indeed, were I a supernaturalist theist, I would feel no need to resist naturalistic explanation.

We bestow meaning rather than discover it. As Aldous Huxley points out in *The Doors of Perception*:

But in so far as we are animals, our business is at all costs to survive. To make biological survival possible, Mind at Large has to be funneled through the reducing valve of the brain and nervous system. What comes out at the other end is a measly trickle of the kind of consciousness which will help us to stay alive on the surface of this particular planet.

The interface between the universe and our perception of it is an open question. All the sexy public debates between celebrity atheists, evangelical pastors, theologians and the like are as meaningless as literary awards and Oscar night. They objectively mean nothing, unless you count the book or ticket sales. The prizes we give ourselves are empty because we humans are both creator, judge and jury. Where is the objective outside observer? If something is called "great" the only real question is "compared to what?"

Mom knew this. She knew that posturing, preening and awarding prizes to ourselves is dust. So Mom stopped in a hotel hallway to change the unhappy life of one hotel maid instead of going to an important meeting with important people. On the other hand she lived out the paradox of being multi-dimensional. Mom also would have *loved* that *New York Times* obit. And she would have positively fawned over Camilla had she met her during her travels. That said, my mother knew what Shakespeare meant by these lines in *Macbeth*:

> *Tomorrow, and tomorrow, and tomorrow,*
> *Creeps in this petty pace from day to day,*
> *To the last syllable of recorded time;*
> *And all our yesterdays have lighted fools*
> *The way to dusty death. Out, out, brief candle!*
> *Life's but a walking shadow, a poor player*

That struts and frets his hour upon the stage
And then is heard no more. It is a tale
Told by an idiot, full of sound and fury,
Signifying nothing.

VI

Lucy and Jack know that I pray every morning on my way down the stairs from my attic bedroom to the studio/office where I write and paint chronicling my garden and the marsh. Sometimes I sit the children up at my easel to paint what they call *real pictures*—oil paintings—"Just like you make, Ba." Sometimes we pray together on the stairs, too, "Just like you, Ba."

"Show me how you pray, Ba," Lucy says from time to time. Standing at the top of the stairs, I demonstrate. "Lord Jesus Christ, son of God," I say, "have mercy upon me, a sinner." Then, "Lord, I offer you this day." As my feet touch each step while I'm descending, I say, "I pray for Genie, Jessica, Francis, John, Amanda, Ben, Dani, Lucy, Jack, Becky and Becky's unborn baby."

When we say grace Jack likes me to ask him to lead us in repeating the Lord's Prayer. Like the "real paintings" they make—compared to the art they make on the floor of the kitchen with poster paints on huge sheets of butcher paper—my grandchildren delight in entering into a grownup spiritual world as equals. Perhaps this is one of the gifts non-religious people have a problem experiencing. They might not meet their children as humble partners in service of something bigger than themselves. How could a non-praying parent get on her knees with a child she's been picking on to confess to that child and beg forgiveness, while in the presence of a larger truth than her own wounded ego? The same goes for churchgoing. Lucy and Jack aren't kids when they are in church. They are fully realized human beings standing in the communion line as equals with the grownups. Thus grownup and child meet, for once, on a level playing field of unknowing.

Sometimes Lucy sits on "her" prayer step. "This is my step, Ba, isn't it?"

I nod. "Yes, that's your step."

The first time Lucy heard me pray for her unborn sister, she said, "You *used* to pray for your writing and painting on the bottom step. Where do you pray for your writing and painting now, Ba?"

"On the top step of the stairs from the second floor landing. Then I ask God to take care of my dead parents, Genie's dead parents, Holly Meade, Francis Ackerman who has Parkinson's, my niece's husband Rodman who has a brain tumor, and my friend Julie Ray, who adopted two little boys out of the foster care system."

When I say grace after Jack and Lucy lead us in the Lord's Prayer, I repeat the names of people I pray for on the stairs. If I forget a name, Jack or Lucy will remind me. The prayers have cemented our family genealogy into their brains. Our prayers have also taught my grandchildren that there are other lives we care about besides our own. If they hear a new name added to the list, they want to know all about that person.

Speaking of friends in need, Lucy and Jack see Francis Ackerman quite often. He stops in for lunch on his way from Augusta, Maine, to his medical checkups in Boston. He's my oldest friend. We met when we were eight years old growing up on the same mountainside in Switzerland. Francis's mother used to come to our chalet for Bible studies and for Sunday lunch. Francis, like me, grew up as the son of expatriate Americans. His dad was a respectable academic, so Francis was less embarrassed than I was when he explained to strangers what his dad did. Living by faith is tough enough to explain to secular (normal!) strangers. Try telling a little girl you meet on the beach—when you're eleven and have a crush on her—what your parents do, when the honest answer is: "Mom and Dad live by faith, which means they pray for God to move the hearts of people to send us money so we can tell the people God calls to the mission of L'Abri about the saving work of Jesus on the cross..." All she had said was, "Daddy's a doctor. What does your father do?"

Francis and I both went to boarding schools in England. We both moved back to the States as adults with our children; Francis to work as the assistant attorney general of Maine, specializing in anti-trust law, and me to Massachusetts to work as a right wing nut who helped launch the Religious Right. After I fled the evangelical world, I became a secular movie director making mediocre R-rated slasher, horror and comedy movies. Then I reinvented myself as a novelist and artist. I returned to my first love of painting only after I'd written many secular books for what—by then—I regarded as "normal readers." (They had mostly never heard of my parents and thus just read my novels for fun.)

Lucy and Jack have seen Francis's health deteriorate. At mealtimes during his visits, Francis sorts through his many pills. Francis has kindly explained his illness to my grandchildren and what each of his pills do. Lucy and Jack always say, "Francis Ackerman, please remember to take your pills so your arms will work!"

Francis's body is freezing up and becoming a cage. And mine? I'm heartbroken. My prayers for Francis have been useless as far as measurable results go.

On the other hand maybe I'm calling the result "useless" because I'm measuring prayer by a universal standard that actually doesn't apply. When we pray for Francis, Lucy and Jack open themselves to something bigger than their own concerns. Our prayers reflect a belief that the universe isn't only about us. Maybe that empathetic concern is something real, rooted into the very fabric of what makes us human. Is the result of the prayer only about Francis's health? Or is prayer for Francis also about the health of everyone who loves him? Perhaps the care and love we feel for Francis reflects a love that predates creation. Perhaps learning the meaning of co-suffering love is the point of the creation experiment.

Predatory illness circles those I love. My niece's husband Rodman has a brain tumor and is supposed to be dead, according to his doctors. When I was back in Switzerland at the family dinner after Mom's funeral, I told Rodman that I was praying for him. He thanked me and wept, though as a former marine he is not a weeping kind of guy. The tumor has played havoc with his emotions. As he wept, he thanked me profusely again and again. All I could think was that if my prayers were keeping him alive then this was one shabby miracle. If God was keeping Rodman barely alive, why not heal him?

Lucy and Jack are too polite to ask why my prayers for Holly's healing failed. They know Francis isn't getting better either. For now, Lucy and Jack seem to accept the fact that we've moved on to "Plan B" for Holly. The good thing about praying for the dead ("Plan B") is that there's no way to test if my prayers are being answered. Nevertheless, Lucy and Jack hear me pray for Mom, Dad, Stan and Betty (Genie's parents) and Holly, though I haven't a clue what God would do *to* these dead people if I failed to pray for them. Am I asking God to protect them from himself, herself or itself? If so, one or all of us are crazy.

I don't believe in hell or heaven, at least not as those places are described in any of the world's scriptures, including the Bible. As a result, trying to picture Holly or Mom or my other relatives or friends in the afterlife (if such a thing exists) is best left comfortingly unspecific. Nevertheless, it feels right, if insane, to pray for them and to talk to them. It even feels normal.

Why does prayer feel both right and normal to me and crazy, too? The best I can do is offer this analogy. In the movie *Close Encounters of the Third Kind,* people receive a vision of a mountain to which they're being called. They don't know what they're seeing, let alone why. They don't believe in callings per se. They just have to go there. In the same way, I just have to pray. And while I know that soon my grandchildren will be asking me tough questions about whether any of this spiritual mumbo-jumbo is real, I'm like a pregnant crack addict passing my addiction to my unborn child. In this case the drug is a spirituality habit I can't kick. I feel compelled to deliver, as it were, yet more prayer babies addicted to spirituality into the world!

I haven't the foggiest idea what prayer *does.* I do know that I can't get through my day without praying. I pray the Orthodox "Jesus Prayer" off and on all day. As if I'm some sort of religiously demented Tourette's sufferer, it prays itself. I wake up with the words in my head, and I fall asleep as this ancient prayer plays in my brain. "Lord Jesus Christ, Son of God, have mercy upon me a sinner" is the inner "sound" that lulls me to sleep. It's as comforting to me as distant surf lapping at the shore. I don't know where this prayer invasion comes from, but I'm thankful to have been invaded.

When I pray, I experience the same sort of optimism I feel when I've just wrapped up a university speaking tour and the plane at last takes off for Boston. My spirits rise. I'll be talking to Genie soon. As we drive home, Genie doesn't have to say anything as I ramble on. It's enough that she listens.

Some conversations are one-way, but they are no less meaningful for all that. When I have a solitary encounter with beauty while on the road, I long to tell Genie. If Genie isn't with me, the painting I see, the movie I watch, the interesting conversation I have doesn't seem to count. It only counts to me when I tell Genie about it. When the words I use fail to tell the story, Genie knows what I *mean* no matter how inadequate my words are. Thus my truest and deepest consciousness resides outside of me in someone else. It's a relief to be understood by someone who knows me better than I know myself.

VII

What began forty-three years ago as sex between teens re-sulting in an unplanned pregnancy—when I said "I'll pull out" I lied!—is winding up as two lovers clinging to each other as if to a life raft. A happy marriage is never entirely happy. I've been a shit sometimes. Now that there's less time ahead of me than behind me, I mostly tell the person I love the truth. The same goes for Genie. We tend to look back over our lives with more mercy than we used to. We are nicer now, or maybe we're just tired.

Over lunch today, Genie told me that looking back at the time when we were living with my family at L'Abri in Switzerland in the 1970s, she feels especially grateful to my parents. Genie was eighteen and I was seventeen when we found she was pregnant. A day after Genie told them her parents called back from San Francisco, and suggested that Genie might want to come home and put our baby up for adoption. By contemplating adoption, completion of college and the launch of a career, Genie's kind parents were doing the sensible loving thing. They told her that whatever else was the case Genie wasn't stuck with me or with a baby. Stan and Betty were so very sensible.

My parents were not sensible. They were crazy fundamental-ists who thought we should get married. Since, unknown to her parents, Genie was actually in love, or thought she was, my parents were telling Genie what she wanted to hear. So she stayed at the mission in Switzerland.

My parents were wrong and right. Their theology of sex and marriage notwithstanding, I think that the real reason they encouraged us to marry was because they loved me. They knew I was in love, wildly infatuated, besotted, and crazily had been proposing to Genie for the better part of six months, ever since she'd strolled into my life. The reality about my parents' view of the "right thing to do" was less about theology and more related to emotion. The emotion was parental love. So Mom and Dad offered us a place to stay, never judged, and helped in any way they could. That "accident" turned out to be our daughter Jessica. She's forty-three years old as I write this, Genie's best friend, and my counselor and confessor. We talk at least once a week on Skype. My world is unthinkable without my daughter.

I don't know if Genie was in love with me when she was the child I married. I know she loves me now. We're still together, though bruised after the years of adjusting to each other and to life while growing up. Genie and I were too young to be parents. Our educations were interrupted and our careers were developed on the fly. Then Jessica grew up and also became a young mother though she waited until she'd married. Jessica's kids Amanda and Ben are older than Genie and I were when we had Jessica.

Jessica also did things backward by today's upper middleclass standards. She dropped out of New York University for love, marriage and childbearing, moved to Finland with her musician/composer husband and only returned to university (in Finland) after her kids were in school. Jessica is still happily married and is now living in Brussels working with the European Union as a successful alternative energy consultant. Yes, I *am* proud of my daughter! So much for my plans! I'm glad I lied and didn't pull out! Sin works out so well sometimes! Hooray for serendipitous messy fate and the ill-advised exchange of body fluids!

Once in a while youthful stupidity is a better way to find happiness than making mature choices. Just ask the sensible forty-something men and women who did the post-graduate-degree/career/wait-for-love-until-the-right-time shuffle and who are scanning dating sites or downloading apps to direct them to the latest date. Some of my friends tell me that they wistfully remember a college or high school sweetheart who they loved but abandoned because, as they put it, "it wasn't the right time for commitment, even though we were in love. I didn't know that would not happen again."

Because Genie and I started a family as teens (no, Amanda, Ben, Jack and Lucy I am *not* advocating this!) our oldest grand-children are the ages of our friends' kids. My beloved Amanda is at the University of Helsinki studying sociology and my beloved Ben is completing high school in Brussels. Only our youngest grandchildren are the ages they're "supposed to be" by today's white, middleclass North American standards. No matter their age, our four (going on five) grandchildren take the sting out of our looming mortality. For Genie and me they are the glue that holds our world together. However we got here, life makes sense when I'm on the floor romping with the grandchildren.

———

We're living in an acquisitive capitalist society that is fundamentally anti-family and fundamentally uncomfortable with just enjoying being human. We'd rather shop than live, acquire than love and stare into a screen than hold each other. The pressure parents put on teenage kids to get into the "right schools" is stressful and cruel. So please forgive me while I preach a little about the joy of children and grandchildren, because plenty of sensible people will tell you to do anything *but* commit to love first and to career, money and possessions second. And this isn't only about heterosexual love. Everything I'm ranting about here is just as true for gay men and lesbian women who are in love and who want children and who like me also want to put their relationships ahead of stuff, prestige and ego. So I have news for us all: it's the *entire* cycle of life that counts. And that cycle is the only real "biological clock" that matters. Everything else is just a footnote.

VIII

Picking up Lucy and Jack from kindergarten and preschool has evolved into a happy ritual. I prepare snacks for them to eat on the way home, usually sliced apples or cheese and crackers for Jack and a banana or black olives and sliced tomatoes for Lucy. The twenty-minute drive home often includes a stop to watch the 1:09 p.m. Newburyport to Boston train hurtle under the bridge on Route 1A. Jack loves trains! When we wave, the driver sounds his bell and blows his horn and Jack shouts, "Hi Joe!" He knows the driver's name from his many visits with Genie to the Newburyport station to watch the trains.

One day just after returning from preschool the grandchildren were in the kitchen painting on butcher paper when a friend phoned. I'll call him "Sam." Sam is a successful movie producer in Hollywood whom I worked with when I was directing movies in the 1980s. Although I quit the movie business in the early 1990s after I wrote *Portofino*, and it was published to rave reviews, thus offering me a passport to a little artistic satisfaction and vindication at last (!), Sam and I are still close friends. We've bickered over our philosophical differences and exchanged visits and insults for years.

Sam asked what I was doing. "I just picked up the grandkids," I said, and without thinking, added, "I love hanging out with the other young mothers at preschool."

Sam paused as he processed my words. "The *other* young mothers?" he said and laughed. "The OTHER young mothers?"

I laughed too, though my remark made sense to me. When I pick up Lucy and Jack, I'm one of the few men and the only grandfather at the preschool. Because Lucy's kindergarten ends half an hour after Jack's preschool, Jack and I have time to play in the hall or outside in the schoolyard while the moms and a few dads come and go.

At first, the mothers couldn't figure me out. Why was this old guy hanging around? Why was he unshaved with unkempt hair, torn jeans and paint all over his clothes? Should someone call the police?

After seeing me every day for a year, the moms know me. Some know I'm a writer and artist, so the paint-spattered look is accepted. One mom checked me out online and discovered I've been interviewed by Oprah and by Terri Gross on NPR's *Fresh Air.* Even a minor celebrity is accorded some eccentric artist slack, at least in the arts-friendly Boston area. I could show up in my bathrobe and slippers and no one would mind. I'm just one of the gang, albeit somewhat of a "character."

The mothers and I discuss one child's cold and how fast the rest of us are likely to catch it. We commiserate about the latest pink eye blight. We talk about one child who wakes up in the night and celebrate the quantum leap another little girl made with her drawing skills after discovering chalk pastels. We note who is pregnant with her second or third child and share strategies for helping a little boy who is scared of pooping because he's sure something is "down there" in the toilet. We congratulate one mom for finally getting a job with health insurance benefits and commiserate with another about the challenging childcare schedule of a night shift nurse.

Some of the mothers are stay-at-home parents while others hurry away from the office at lunchtime to meet their child, deliver her to the babysitter and race back to work. Some have told me about problems with teenage stepchildren, previous marriages, divorces and their struggles to fit into New England after moving from a "friendlier part of the country." Some moms arrive in old cars while others drive new SUVs. No matter what we drive or earn, or if we're married, black, brown or white, single, gay, heterosexual or divorced, when we get down on our knees at eye-level with our babies as they run into our arms, we understand each other perfectly.

The child we're meeting touches the core of our being. Every mom delights in the pint-sized human shouting, "Hi, Mommy!"

The shouted greeting that makes my heart skip is "Hi, Ba!"

Our shared experience of vulnerability erases the age and gender differences between the young mothers and me. We share a fearful solidarity; call it the flip side of love. If anything awful were to happen to the child clambering into our arms, the universe, as we know it, would end.

———

Sam, the ever self-consciously tolerant embodiment of liberal open mindedness, wouldn't have minded my doing a little gender bending or even cross-dressing. But hanging out with ordinary women at a preschool is a long way from "giving good meeting" with the right people in Hollywood. Childcare isn't a sexy job in America and *grandparent* and *aging* are downright scary words.

Sam wanted some reassurance that I was still writing and hadn't given up on my literary career to "take care of someone else's kids," as he called *my* grandchildren. "Haven't you already raised your family? Can't they just get a babysitter or something?"

"Are you kidding me?" I said. "This is the only thing I've ever done I feel entirely happy about." What I said next was illogical, but after calling myself a young mom, why not give Sam something to *really* shake his head over? So I shouted, "Jesus liked hanging out with women and kids too! *So fuck you!*"

Luckily, Beethoven's Fourth Piano Concerto was playing so loudly that Lucy and Jack didn't hear me. Sam and I laughed, and when we stopped laughing Sam yelled "Stop proselytizing!"

Sam knows I grew up as a missionary kid. According to the theology I grew up with, he likes to joke that he's one of the lost. He asks me if I shouldn't be doing more to get him saved since my parents would have urged me to witness to him, or as Mom would have put it, to "share the gospel with your unsaved Jewish friend." (I don't think my parents would have thought my yelling at Sam to go fuck himself because Jesus liked children counts as sharing the gospel.)

Sam frets about religion while he claims to be an atheist. So as the children painted, Sam and I continued our decades-long "discussion" or as Jack once called it, after overhearing several phone calls, our decades-long "yelling at your friend." Sam observed that Ricky Jay (a magician, actor, writer and sleight-of-hand artist revered for his card tricks, memory feats and amusing literate stage patter) could have been proclaimed Messiah, too, "if Ricky had shown up in Judea with a pack of cards."

Sam and I have teased one another for twenty years-plus with politically incorrect and religiously loaded jibes related to his self-described atheism and my escape from the evangelical world. It gets complicated, though, because my escape ended in yet another religious captivity and his atheism is theologically obsessed. Sam knows that twenty-five years ago I joined the Greek Orthodox Church as part of my rebellion against my evangelical past. Ironically, I left one church only to reinvent myself as another kind of churchgoer. And I know that for an atheist Sam seems to want to discuss theology way too much.

I'm just as inconsistent. I go to my local Greek Orthodox church with Lucy and Jack because I feel guilty if I don't. I no longer fool myself into thinking this is about belief. I know my religious expression is about *need*. I don't feel guilty if I don't take my grandchildren because I think church services will save them but because the Liturgy is a beautiful experience of a larger reality than that offered by our shabby materialist utilitarian culture. Okay, that's bullshit. Actually, I'd feel guilty because Mom and Dad conditioned me to be in church on Sunday!

On the other hand to the extent I choose to go, church is one of the places I may offer my grandchildren a vision of a life that is about more than status, stuff, education and money. I go to church with the kids for the same reason Genie and I play our grandchildren classical music and litter the floors and chairs all over our home with open art books. Jack, age three, eats his lunch with a big Goya book propped in front of him asking for the pictures he wants to see. You haven't lived until you've seen a three-year-old boy with his mouth full of cheese and crackers; mumble, "Ba, show me the *Nude Maja* and *Clothed Maja*, please." The best part of any day is watching Jack earnestly studying Goya's clothed model, in contrast to her famous nude mirror image, and asking for the tenth time, "But Ba, *why* didn't she get dressed after her bath?"

Sam still calls me a religious nut and asks me about religious issues as if asking for reports from an exotic planet. I'm his token believer. He's fascinated that I was raised evangelical, became my evangelist father's sidekick for a while in the 1970s and early 80s, traveled the heartland of the American Religious Right and then fled. (I'm the only person he knows who was a regular on the early days of the *700 Club!*)

Sam reveres the *New York Times* the way evangelicals revere the Bible. When they published a profile of me following the publication of my memoir *Crazy for God*, Sam decided that all the stories I'd told him over the years about how nutty my childhood was must be true. The *Times* said so! Maybe Jerry Falwell really *did* lend me his jet in the early 1980s so I could visit his school and preach a sermon from his pulpit. And Sam loved reading that my former evangelical "friends" consider me a traitor to God and to my family, even though I'm still religious and go to church. He even dug up a review of my memoir published in an evangelical magazine that didn't challenge the facts I'd presented about the rise of the Religious Right and my family's involvement in it, but rather denounced me as having committed "the sin of Noah's sons" (no kidding!) because I'd candidly written about the fact that my father was far less than perfect.

Sam called me and said, "I mean are you people complete morons or what? You 'sinned' so your book is shit? All writers are jerks! So there are no good books already? What's with demonizing you instead of taking on your main point?"

"Sam," I said, "you have a lot to learn. How else can they defend their make-believe?"

IX

S am likes to call me out of the blue and casually mention the latest dumb stunt perpetrated by the Religious Right, the Roman Catholic bishops or the Republican Party, as if I have anything to do with it. He pretends I'm still one of "them" whenever "they" do something insane. A televangelist says gay people are going to hell... A bunch of bishops try to ban women from getting insurance coverage for contraceptives... Sam is on the phone!

I like those nutty right-wing stunts. They're why people like Rachel Maddow invite me onto cable news programs. My commentary goes something like this:

Rachel: "Frank, you used to be one of them so tell us, how dumb are these people?"

Me: "Very dumb, Rachel."

Rachel: "How dangerous are they?"

Me: "Very dangerous. Buy my new book and you'll know why!"

It's a living... of sorts.

Kidding with Sam takes a liturgical, ritualistic form, just like my "How-dumb-are-they" routine on cable news shows. Sam stands in for all the "typical, liberal secular Jews," and I tease him about being overly politically correct or ask him what the word *Jew* means when it's combined with the word *secular*.

"Doesn't that confirm that Zionism really is just racism?" I say. "If being a Jew is just a cultural or racial matter, then what right did you all have to steal Palestine from the Palestinians?" Sam retorts by calling evangelical right-wingers "you people."

———

Sam didn't get a rise out of me when he said that Ricky Jay could have been proclaimed as the Messiah because I happened to agree with him. "Another day," I said, "another prophet doing tricks in a part of the world hooked on magical thinking. Besides, Sam, you know I'm not sure if God exists. So don't bust my chops about Jesus' miracles! The only reason I still think Jesus means anything is that even the people writing the gospels disapproved of his actions."

Sam went off to his next meeting and I ran a bath for the children. I was still preoccupied with the things I should have said, like every time Jesus mentioned the Torah, he qualified it with something like this: "The scriptures say thus and so, but I say…"

I *should* have said, "Jesus undermined the inerrancy of the scriptures in favor of his version of pragmatic empathy!" or "Every time Jesus undermined the scriptures it was to err on the side of non-judgmental co-suffering love. So up yours, Sam!"

———

A leper came to Jesus and said, "Lord, if you choose, you can make me clean." If Jesus had been a good religious Jew, he would have said, "Be healed," and just walked away. Instead, he stretched out his hand and touched the leper, saying, "I do choose. Be made clean," even though he was breaking the specific rules of Leviticus. Two chapters teach that anyone touching a person with leprosy is contaminated.

Jesus certainly was *not* a "Bible believer," as we use that term in the post Billy Graham era of American fundamentalist religiosity that's used as a trade-marked product to sell religion. Jesus didn't take the Jewish scriptures at face value. In fundamentalist terms, Jesus was a rule-breaking relativist who wasn't even "saved," according to evangelical standards. Evangelicals insist that you have to believe very specific interpretations of the Bible to be saved. Jesus didn't. He undercut the scriptures.

The stories about Jesus that survived the bigots, opportunists and delusional fanatics who wrote the New Testament contain powerful and enlightened truths that would someday prove the undoing of the Church built in his name. Like a futurist vindicated by events as yet undreamed, Jesus' message of love was far more powerful than the magical thinking of the writers of the book he's trapped in. In Jesus' day the institutions of religion, state, misogyny and myth were so deeply ingrained that the ultimate dangerousness of his life example could not be imagined. For example his feminism, probably viewed as an eccentricity in his day, would prove transformational.

Jesus believed *in* God rather than in a book *about* God. The message of Jesus' life is an intervention in and an acceleration of the evolution of empathy. Consider this story from the book of Matthew: "A woman who had been subject to bleeding for twelve years came up behind him and touched the edge of his cloak. She said to herself, 'If I only touch his cloak, I will be healed.' Jesus turned and saw her. 'Take heart, daughter,' he said, 'your faith has healed you.' And the woman was healed at that moment."

Jesus recognized a bleeding woman touching him as a sign of her faith. By complimenting rather than rebuking her, Jesus ignored another of his scripture's rules: "If a woman has a discharge of blood for many days, not at the time her [period], or if she has a discharge beyond the time, all the days of her discharge she shall continue in uncleanness... Every bed on which she lies during all the days of her discharge shall be treated as [unclean]... Everything on which she sits shall be unclean ... Whoever touches these things shall be unclean" (Leviticus 15:25).

Jesus' un-first-century antics went beyond coddling lepers and welcoming the touch of a bleeding woman. He held a dead girl's hand, violating explicit commands: "He shall not go in to any dead bodies nor make himself unclean, even for his father or for his mother" (Leviticus 21:11) and "Whosoever toucheth the dead body of any man that is dead, and purifieth not himself, defileth the tabernacle of the LORD; and that soul shall be cut off from Israel: because the water of separation was not sprinkled upon him, he shall be unclean; his uncleanness is yet upon him" (Numbers 19:13).

As an ultimate fuck you to rule-keeping scripture zealots everywhere, Jesus hung out with whores. Embracing whores was a double rebuke to the Jewish scripture-thumpers because it put Jesus on the side of the pagan, prostitute-condoning Roman occupiers and made him a traitor in the culture wars of the day. Yet, the anointing of Jesus by a prostitute is one of the few events reported in all four gospels. As Jesus blessed and defended her, Matthew's gospel says the disciples "were indignant" while Luke describes the woman who did the anointing as "a woman in that town who lived a sinful life," which is a coded phrase for a filthy hooker who is certainly *not* one of *us*.

Jesus' embrace of a woman from an enemy tribe in a culture where tribal belonging was paramount distressed both his followers and enemies. His attitude to the "other" was as incomprehensible as if he'd blurted "$E=mc^2$ is the equation of mass–energy equivalence." The Samaritan woman at the well knew that his actions were shocking. When Jesus stopped to talk to her, she said, "You are a Jew and I am a Samaritan woman. How can you ask me for a drink? For Jews do not associate with Samaritans" (John 4:9).

Jesus responded by attacking the preeminence of religion and group identity, offering an entirely new way of looking at spirituality by emphasizing basic human dignity above nation, state, gender or religion:

> "Sir," the woman said, "I can see that you are a prophet. Our ancestors worshiped on this mountain, but you Jews claim that the place where we must worship is in Jerusalem."
>
> "Woman," Jesus replied, "believe me, a time is coming when you will worship the Father neither on this mountain nor in Jerusalem. You Samaritans worship what you do not know; we worship what we do know, for salvation is from the Jews. Yet a time is coming and has now come when the true worshipers will worship the Father in the Spirit and in truth, for they are the kind of worshipers the Father seeks. God is spirit, and his worshipers must worship in the Spirit and in truth" (John 4:19–24).

Jesus rejects tribalism, literalism, group identity, specific religions, and gatekeepers as well as his Jewish identity. The phrase "Salvation is from the Jews" is paradoxically a reference to his liberating departure from tribal identity in favor of common humanity.

What is the implication of Jesus-centric non-theological, non-dogmatic salvation? It's the *abolishing* of exclusion of the other as "unsaved."

What about God? Jesus says that God doesn't want (or maybe no longer wants) worship via exclusionary religion, sacrifice or membership in the correct tribe, sect or nation. No, Jesus says, the Father *wants* "true worshipers [who] will worship the Father in the Spirit and in truth."

In other words Jesus decouples the credulous attachment to a tribal geography and religion-based identity. Jesus declares we're all one family. Goodbye, Abrahamic covenant, Jerusalem, Mecca, Rome and Constantinople. *Au revoir*, holy places, River Ganges, passports, borders, empires, Lourdes, clan, tribe, Hellenism, Russian imperial ambition *and* American exceptionalism. No more chants of "USA! USA!" for, "a time is coming and has now come when the true worshipers will worship the Father in the Spirit and in truth." According to Jesus, there never was and never will be a "greatest country on earth," or a "city set on a hill" or a "chosen people."

X

Jesus' contemporaries were horrified that he had female friends. In the Luke story about Mary and Martha, Martha stayed out of sight working in the kitchen as do many Middle Eastern women even today. Jesus invited Martha to forgo her female role and join Mary to sit with him in the living room.

The stories about Jesus' respect for women as equals of men made their way into an otherwise disgustingly misogynistic Bible. The Bible's editors assembled the final canon of the Christian scriptures by about the year 400 and probably only included such stories as Jesus blessing a whore for anointing him, or meeting and talking with the Samaritan woman because they couldn't omit them without their book losing credibility. The Bible was edited in a cultural context where oral tradition was sacrosanct. The gospel stories had been *told* again and again long before they were written down. The Bible's editors must have cringed at having to include them.

Jesus was such a mess! He was far less moralistic than the apostles, let alone St. Paul. The Bible's editors included letters by men such as St. Paul, telling women to essentially shut up. In First Corinthians, 14:33-34-35, Paul wrote: "As in all the congregations of the saints, women should remain silent in the churches. They are not allowed to speak, but must be in submission, as the Law says. If they want to inquire about something, they should ask their own husbands at home; for it is disgraceful for a woman to speak in the church."

Jesus told Martha to come out of the kitchen and *talk to him.* Jesus' behavior clashes with not just the Bible but also with our misogynistic culture in which women themselves even collaborate in the oppression of other women. Oppression is most powerful when internalized and self-imposed. Self-oppression (knowing your "place") becomes a passport to acceptance by the dominant group. Sometime fundamentalist women perpetrate crimes against their daughters by training them to act subservient to males. Sometimes thoroughly modern secular "feminists" also betray other women. A multi-billion-dollar fashion industry run by powerful men and women preys on women's insecurities to convince them to buy its products. A darker side is exposed when young people with body-image issues starve themselves to death to emulate the wraith-like models in fashion magazines

Then there's medically sanctioned cutting for profit. Can a woman (or man) live happily if she (or he) has the "wrong" body type? Slice! What about a woman with normal signs of aging? Slice! Cosmetic and plastic surgery are growth industries.

Highly lucrative marketing campaigns exploit the strongest evolutionary command hardwired into human primates: *reproduction.* The use of youth, sex and, by implication, fertility as an advertising tool targets women disproportionately. The multibillion dollar fashion/cosmetics/surgery industry reinforces sexual insecurity.

In advertising mythology, gorgeous females attract virile males because they wear or use the right products. Buy this and you will be a totally fulfilled human being! You're one handbag, Mercedes, or smart phone away from nirvana! But are people fulfilled and accepted when they faithfully emulate the advertisers' glossy dreamscape? No, not even the beautiful people are ever quite beautiful enough. Jesus said as much: "Woe unto you, scribes and Pharisees, hypocrites! for ye are like unto whited sepulchers, which indeed appear beautiful outward, but are within full of dead men's bones, and of all uncleanness" (Matthew 23:27). This will never be the favorite Bible quote of *Vogue* magazine editors nor, I suspect, of monks and priests dressing up in holy costumes and acting the part of confessors while imposing themselves (and too often their sexual hang-ups) between the faithful and God.

———

The impact of Jesus' feminism has yet to be fully realized. Even famous women receive an extraordinary amount of abuse. Women are attacked with sexual innuendo and threats of sexual violence online. Feminists who ask for basic respect and equality are belittled. If a woman calls out gender bias, she is likely to hear, "strident bitch with no sense of humor!" In our culture, an admirably strong woman is deemed "not a lady." Being seen as nurturing is also seen as a political weakness, even by some women. Genie sometimes runs into women who behave as condescendingly to her as Sam did to me when they find out she's "only doing" childcare for our grandchildren. If Genie wants respect from a certain kind of woman or man steeped in the values of our capitalist consumer society, she must also point out that she's a publisher who owns her own company.

In the never-say-never category of complexity trumping prejudice, my experience as a "mom" has led to my discussing the role of women here. Paradox abounds. Delaying pregnancy is one indicator that a woman will usually have some independence, but Genie and I broke this rule and Genie is a happy, fulfilled woman. We got away with our stupidity because we had enough love and support for Genie to reinvent herself *while* we figured out how to be parents. We were lucky, but even more important, we were loved.

Paradoxically, that unconditional love happened *to us* in an Evangelical mission context filled with people most atheists would denounce as backward bigots—only they weren't. And yet, Genie's and my happy experience aside, two thousand years after Jesus treated women as equals, countless fundamentalist American parents are preparing their daughters to forgo personal goals and accept subservient roles in marriages better suited to first-century Israel. It can seem as if Jesus failed to change anything.

XI

I hate to be the bearer of bad news to anyone hooked on apocalyptic fantasies, but things are getting better. Jesus did in fact change everything.

For all our massive failings, Christianity redefined the classical ideal of the worth of the individual. The inclusion of "others" is the greatest ethical insight of Christianity because tribalism and excluding classes of people is the enemy of justice. Even thugs pay lip service to human rights these days. And in some places those rights are actually protected.

Two millennia after Jesus taught, Christ-like change is beginning to infuse the world at many levels more widely than ever before. So why does it seem as if so many Christians still fail to grasp the essential truth of our faith: inclusion and justice? Maybe our blindness started when the first Christians didn't believe what Jesus told them about the kingdom of God: "Neither shall they say, Lo here! Or, lo there! For, behold, the kingdom of God is *within you*" (Luke 17:21, *emphasis* added). Irrespective of Jesus' teaching we continue to tie faith to doctrine, geography, nation, male prerogatives, homophobia and race. It is as if we've rewritten Jesus' saying as: "They *shall* say, Lo here! And, Lo there! For, behold, the kingdom of God *is only found in correct doctrine believed by the chosen few of our tribe!*"

Jesus took the long view. "He presented another parable to them, saying, 'The kingdom of heaven is like a mustard seed, which a man took and sowed in his field; and this is smaller than all other seeds, but when it is full grown, it is larger than the garden plants and becomes a tree, so that *the birds of the air* come and *nest in its branches*'" (Matthew 13:31-32).

Jesus built what I think of as an empathy time bomb. He lit a slow-burning fuse—then left. Whatever you believe about *how* Jesus left—be it via death, resurrection or flying into the clouds—*what* he left behind remains: the accelerated pace of the evolution of our ethical consciousness. Essentially Jesus said: To hell with mere survival *Choose* to evolve into a new and better animal!

What Jesus triggered was an inexorable shift to a higher level of ethics that eventually changed the trajectory of human history. Love, fairness, opportunity, freedom and goodness eventually begin to trump mere survival and brute power.

Does that mean that Jesus only achieved social change? I hope not! I *hope* that Jesus was born in order to show me how to better love God. But as I understand it, the spiritual reconciliation where we learn to worship in spirit, as Jesus said, has a practical side.

Our image of God-the-judgmental-deranged-monster badly needed fixing. Jesus came to edit our ideas. Part of Jesus' teaching was to redirect our attention to serving a loving God by serving others. We needed to see God anew through Jesus because our conception of God, as expressed in all religious texts including in our Bible, made him, her, or it out to be a retributive fiend championing the side of his chosen.

In order to understand how to serve a God who no longer demanded sacrifice, killing and revenge, we need to listen again to Jesus' radical definition of faith. As recorded in Matthew 25: 34-40, Jesus' updated humane God wants mercy above sacrifice and compassion above moralism.

> "Then the King will say to those on his right, 'Come, you who are blessed by my Father; take your inheritance, the kingdom prepared for you since the creation of the world. For I was hungry and you gave me something to eat, I was thirsty and you gave me something to drink, I was a stranger and you invited me in, I needed clothes and you clothed me, I was sick and you looked after me, I was in prison and you came to visit me.'
>
> Then the righteous will answer him, 'Lord, when did we see you hungry and feed you, or thirsty and give you something to drink? When did we see you a stranger and invite you in, or needing clothes and clothe you? When did we see you sick or in prison and go to visit you?'
>
> The King will reply, 'Truly I tell you, whatever you did for one of the least of these brothers and sisters of mine, you did for me.'"

XII

The humanist Enlightenment was the catalyst for Jesus' empathy time bomb, the message of inclusion for the excluded. The Enlightenment came to Europe through philosophers like Voltaire who were influenced by the ethics Jesus taught. Eventually these ethics—as reinterpreted by secular Enlightenment philosophers—caused countries like Denmark, Sweden, Finland, Holland and Norway to become places where being young, female, sick or old isn't such a bad thing.

The Anglo-Saxon world also felt what I call the emancipating Jesus time bomb effect. Feminist themes were emerging in Western religious culture before secular feminism emerged as a movement. The drive for the abolition of slavery in the United States was often led by women, some of whom also argued for the right of women to lead churches. Many nineteenth-century women in the States and Britain including Lucy Stone and Antoinette Brown graduated from schools like Charles Finney's Oberlin College in Ohio, the first college in the US to admit women and blacks. Brown was the first woman in the US to be ordained. (Even before that, the Wesleyan revival in Britain included female leaders. Margaret Fell, a Quaker, argued for the right of women to preach.)

Nineteenth-century women first gained power in non-conformist denominations by arguing *the example of Jesus*. They gained power in these churches *before* the secular society gave them the vote or modern secular feminism arose in the post-World War II period.

Marxism influenced feminism as well, viewing both established religion and the economic systems it endorsed as oppressive. Marxist feminists castigated patriarchal religion in exploiting women even though Marxism itself was a form of Christian heresy unlikely to have arisen outside the Jesus-saturated West. Marx denounced religion as hypocritical *because* Jesus advocated helping the poor while the establishment Christian church emulated the earlier oppressive Roman state.

As French philosopher, law professor and sociologist Jacques Ellul writes in his introduction to *Jesus and Marx: From Gospel to Ideology* (1988).

> Clearly the first step is to question Christian ideology itself: Christianity as power and as ideology. In this connection we see that Karl Marx's and Friedrich Nietzsche's criticisms, for example, are clearly on target... But it would be much better for Christians themselves to do this work. All we must do is get on with criticizing our own ideas, convictions, churches, and movements on the basis of a demanding rather than a rationalizing reading of the Bible. This means we must renounce reading the Bible to find arguments to justify our behavior or that of our group. Any time we read the Bible to find arguments or justifications, we wallow in Christian ideology.

Neither Marxist nor Christian feminism is possible to imagine without the Enlightenment just as the Enlightenment is impossible to envision other than as a reaction to the hypocrisy of the, establishment Church. The Church clearly failed to live by Jesus' enlightened and rational grasp of human brotherhood and sisterhood. The call of the Enlightenment was toward a rational basis for living and thinking that held no tradition too sacred to question.

Jesus was the first of the Enlightenment philosophers. In John 8: 4-7 speaking like some sort of first century Voltaire, Jesus questioned the laws and traditions of his day. "And the scribes and Pharisees brought unto him a woman taken in adultery; and when they had set her in the midst, they said to him, 'Master, this woman was taken in adultery, in the very act. Now Moses in the law commanded us, that such should be stoned: but what sayest thou?' ... Jesus said unto them, 'He that is without sin among you, let him first cast a stone at her.'" Voltaire couldn't have said it better.

As a Christian heresy that strove to fulfill the greatest promises of the inner kingdom of God as preached and lived by Jesus, the Enlightenment writers put human non-exclusionary justice ahead of the law. This rational philosophy did not condemn according to a set of rules but demanded moral consistency and compassion from those who would judge.

Enlightenment thinkers jettisoned the ugly, exclusionary and magical parts of the religion that grew up bearing Christ's name. Their goal was what Ellul called on the Church to do in *Jesus and Marx*: "On all levels and in every aspect of our society, the poor are rejected, mistreated, and forced more deeply into their poverty. *Christianity should have taken up the cause of the poor; better yet, it should have identified with the poor.* Instead, during almost the entire course of its history, the Church has served as a prop of the powerful and has been on the side of exploiters and states" (emphasis in original).

Christ-imitating social enlightenment arose from the New Testament ethos, but rarely through the established Church. The Enlightenment thinkers were denounced as heretics. Secularists and deists, the very people the Church most hated and feared formed and articulated Enlightenment policies. Thus Jesus' prophetic theme of a building founded on the corner stone "rejected by the builders" (Psalm 118:22) continued replicating in the humanist Enlightenment. *In spite* of being largely rejected by the Church a new Jesus-leavened order was born.

Voltaire, the French Enlightenment writer, historian and philosopher, attacked the injustice of aristocratic privilege, the brutality of war, and the dogmatic mentality of the Church. He launched his attacks *by contrasting the words and ideology of the Church with those of Jesus*. Writing on deism, Voltaire argued that true religion "does not consist either in the opinions of an unintelligible metaphysic, or in vain display, but in worship and justice." Similarly, his essay on religion contrasts institutional religion with the lived religion of the greatest commandment as Voltaire engages with Jesus ("a man of gentle, simple countenance") in a dream-like fantasy:

> I saw a man of gentle, simple countenance, who seemed to me to be about thirty-five years old... I was astonished to find his feet swollen and bleeding, his hands likewise, his side pierced, and his ribs flayed with whip cuts... I said to him, "is it possible for a just man, a sage, to be in this

state?... Is it by priests and judges that you have been so cruelly assassinated?"

He answered with much courtesy—"Yes."

"And who were these monsters?"

"They were hypocrites."

"Ah! That says everything. I understand by this single word that they must have condemned you to death… You wanted to teach them a new religion, then?"

"Not at all; I said to them simply—'Love God with all your heart and your fellow-creature as yourself, for that is man's whole duty.'"

XIII

Although the Enlightenment philosophers' followers rejected the institutional Church and the brutal hypocrites who
ran it, they were among the first to challenge society to actually
carry out Jesus' vision of compassionate humanism on a large,
transformative scale. Many died for speaking truth to power.
Count Johann Friedrich Struensee (1737-1772) was killed for
trying to follow Jesus, and also, since nothing is ever simple, for
sleeping with the king's wife.

Born in Germany to Pietist pastor and theologian Adam
Struensee, Johann became a doctor and a follower of Voltaire
and Jean-Jacques Rousseau. State-endorsed religious leaders
feared Pietist doctrine because Pietists had no reverence for
state churches. The leaders of the state churches viewed these
"nonconformist churches" as a danger to the social order and
to their own power. Struensee was thus shaped by his religious
family's outsider status in Germany.

Through a fluky series of circumstances, Struensee got to try
out his Enlightenment ideas on a large scale. As physician to
King Christian VII of Denmark, he became regent of Denmark
when the king's life-long mental illness grew extreme enough
to create a power vacuum. Struensee's dramatic social reforms
included universal health care, limits on the totalitarian power

of the Church, abolishing torture, removing censorship of the press, revoking privileges for nobles, introducing luxury taxes to fund the care of orphans, banning the slave trade and abolishing capital punishment.

The Roman Catholic hierarchy and their government minister allies fought against Struensee's reforms through a campaign designed to arouse public sentiment against the reformer. When he had an affair with Queen Caroline Matilda, Struensee provided his enemies with just what they needed to get rid of him. On the pretext that he had "usurped the royal authority," he was tried for treason, found guilty and tortured to death with the blessing of the Church. His enemies quickly overturned his visionary reforms, but could not snuff out the fuse Struensee had relit on Jesus' empathy bomb.

If Struensee returned to Denmark today, he'd find a society practicing the reforms he fought for. Yet American evangelicals would deem most of the compassionate citizens of Denmark—who are living according to Jesus' teaching about how to treat people—as "godless" and try to send American missionaries.

Fewer than 5 percent of Danes attend church. In godless Denmark, the national government funds a high quality education for all children, rich and poor alike, while in God-fearing America, education is funded through local property taxes, so neighborhood and income dictate a child's educational opportunities. Add in race and ethnicity factors to create a perfectly stratified school system segregated by educational opportunity.

The godless Danes insist on paying their public school teachers well and according them prestige. No wonder teaching in Denmark is a competitive job attracting the best and brightest men and women. Since the 1950s when church-going America saw increasing numbers of women drawn to teaching, salaries dropped, educational standards fell and advancement opportunities stagnated. Danish university students receive a stipend to help complete their studies while their American peers incur large debts.

Danish policy initiatives for supporting families include flexible working hours, universal childcare, parental leave and generous benefits. Godless Denmark mandates four weeks of maternity leave before childbirth and fourteen weeks afterward for mothers. Parents of newborn children are assisted with well-baby nurse-practitioner visits in their homes. In the "pro-life" and allegedly "family friendly" American Bible belt, conservative political leaders slash programs designed to help women and children while creating a justifying mythology about handouts versus empowerment. In God-fearing America the poor are now the "takers," no longer the "least of these," and many conservative evangelicals side with today's Pharisees, attacking the poor in Jesus' name.

———

Who then are Jesus' followers: the secular, godless Danes caring for the poor or the don't-tread-on-me Ayn Rand-inspired libertarians and their church-going enablers? And for all the talk about the "real America" bandied about by right wingers, the humanistic impact of Jesus' thinking was central to America's founding. The Declaration of Independence is an Enlightenment document containing the words "All men are created equal," a direct extension of Jesus' inclusive vision. Lincoln built on this idea in his Gettysburg Address.

We have Jesus and his Enlightenment prophets to thank for the humanistic ideas on which America was founded. If you're one of the people Jesus is said to have favored—a child, a woman, someone ill, a sex worker, someone regarded as untouchable, old, ugly, abandoned or "the other" in some other way—and you are being cared for by unbelievers, is Jesus' example being followed? Or does Jesus only live in correct theology regardless of how little a Christian may care about your wellbeing?

XIV

At 4 a.m. I interrupted my writing and stepped out of my studio office to pee on the grass. I like the sensation of cold dew under my bare feet, so I adjusted my bathrobe, stared skyward at the stars and crescent moon and, not for the first or last time, thought that we're spouting nonsense when humans talk about traveling to outer space.

We're *already* hurtling through outer space clinging to a spaceship while breathing the thin bubble of air that surrounds us. Our water and air is protected by a magnetic field deflecting a solar wind that would otherwise strip away everything that supports life, as it did on Mars. We grow food on our spaceship, busy ourselves with life onboard and rarely consider that we know neither where our journey began nor our destination. We're also traveling at a speed of 2,236,000 miles per hour towards a structure we humans have named the Great Attractor, a region of space some 150 million light years away.

To talk about going to outer space is to indulge in the same kind of delusional thinking captured by a headline describing an impenetrable fog blanketing the British Isles: "Fog in Channel: Continent Cut Off." Whether real or apocryphal, the headline is the epitome of provincialism. The tiny island of Britain is portrayed as the geographical reference point for the entire continent of Europe in the same way that we humans once thought of ourselves as occupying the center of our universe.

In AD 150 Ptolemy of Alexandria described an Earth-centric astronomical system with moon, sun, planets and stars revolving around us, formalizing beliefs central to Greco-Roman myth. The god Helios supposedly drove the chariot of the sun across the sky while Earth stood still. The Bible reinforced this geocentric fallacy. Psalm 19 states: "In the heavens [God] has set a tabernacle for the sun, which comes forth like a bridegroom leaving his chamber and like a strong man runs its course with joy. Its rising is from the end of the heavens and its circuit to the end of them."

As my son Francis reminded me when giving me his generous and helpful notes for this book, the geocentric model only superficially glorified humankind while actually denigrating it. Place Earth in the center and "down" serves to locate sin. Humans were "down here," separate from good things located "up there." According to Dante, Satan was trapped by sin at the center of Earth. The geography of the universe externalized the geography of sin, locating humankind firmly "down here." This idea was so universally fixed that Newton's idea of gravity seemed laughable to some otherwise smart people. As Francis scrawled in the margin of this book's manuscript, "Educated contemporaries of Newton wondered how there could be two 'downs' or centers of attraction. Did sin or gravity 'hold' everything together? The mind boggles!"

———

Now we've all been put in our place. The United Kingdom is just another country in the European Union, the so-called biblical cosmology has been debunked, and Copernicus and Galileo have been vindicated. To rephrase the headline, it's we humans who are now cut off. We're constantly reminded that Earth is insignificant and situated at the far edge of an ordinary galaxy. When I typed the words "Earth's place in the universe" into a search engine, many answers similar to the one published on the London Natural History Museum's website popped up: "With a circumference of over 40,000 kilometers, the Earth feels very large. In relation to our solar system, our galaxy and beyond it is in fact tiny... Our place within the universe is very small and insignificant."

But what do the words *far away, tiny, significant* or *insignificant* mean in the context of forever? To rate Earth's place as tiny and insignificant in relation to things we label huge, vast and significant is as absurd as assigning Michelin restaurant ratings based on the weight of a restaurant or the number of tiles on its kitchen wall. If the words "Our place within the universe is very small and insignificant" were to have any meaning, we would have to be able to define the word *significant.*

Smaller than *what? Less significant* than *what?* Where's the standard of universal normal kept?

"Our place within the universe is very small and insignificant" is as subjective a statement as Lucy telling me that the sun is as big as a tree. It's as nonsensical and theological in nature as the claims of truth made by Pope Paul V in 1616 when he threatened Galileo and abjured him "to abandon completely... the opinion that the Sun stands still at the center of the world and the earth moves, and henceforth not to hold, teach, or defend it in any way whatever, either orally or in writing."

The pope, as if foreshadowing the famed real estate mantra, defended medieval Christian beliefs about humanity's God-given significance by arguing that value is derived from one thing only: location, location, *location.*

Apparently, the London Natural History Museum is also stuck on the significance of location. They defend a post-Christian article of faith in human *insignificance* that is based on physical location, size and place in relation to other celestial bodies.

It's not enough to merely defend or denigrate our location as the defining truth about our significance, the state of our souls is also on trial! To the secular doctrine of human insignificance has been added a secular version of Original Sin. Humankind's sins against Earth's ecological well-being nicely mirror the earlier theology of our fall and our banishment from the mythical Eden. We may have left religion behind, but once again, we're being taught that we're guilty simply for being born. John Calvin would be delighted.

Today's secular science of human insignificance inspires its own theology. This secular theology assigns us a contradictory groveling *insignificant, significance.* We have evolved to a high enough level of ethical consciousness to understand that we're guilty as charged, and are merely insignificant and yet, morally culpable destroyers of life.

We may not be saying "Lord have mercy" so often these days, but we're still muttering "I'm unworthy!" As with past theology, a vast *oeuvre* of secular iconic art is dedicated to keeping us in our place. The old and new theologies of significant insignificance share joylessness. Hell awaits the backslidden unbeliever of old, and the extinction of life awaits modern-day polluters. A certain gleeful delight at our awaiting comeuppance seems to characterize both the old and new prophets calling for repentance.

Speaking of secular icons… in the early twentieth century Marcel Duchamp hung a porcelain urinal on an art gallery wall to debunk the pretentions of art and the pretensions of human significance. Duchamp created this work entitled "Fountain" in order to (as he put it) "de-deify" art. Carl Sagan did the same thing for cosmology when he wrote *Pale Blue Dot: A Vision of the Human Future in Space*. Sagan played for higher stakes than Duchamp had. He attempted to "de-deify" our entire species. His beautiful, secular psalm dedicated to our demotion is unsurpassed. In Psalm 8, King David described us as only a little lower than the angels while in *Pale Blue Dot*, Sagan takes great pains to obliterate any sense of cosmic significance:

> We succeeded in taking that picture and, if you look at it, you see a dot. That's here. That's home. That's us. On it everyone you know, everyone you love, everyone you've ever heard of, every human being who ever was, lived out their lives. The aggregate of all our joys and sufferings, thousands of confident religions, ideologies and economic doctrines. Every hunter and forager, every hero and coward, every creator and destroyer of civilizations, every king and peasant, every young couple in love, every hopeful child, every mother and father, every inventor and explorer, every teacher of morals, every corrupt politician, every superstar, every supreme leader, every saint and sinner in the history of our species, lived there—on a mote of dust suspended in a sunbeam.

Yet even post-Duchamp and post-Sagan, we value life so highly that we seek it elsewhere in the universe as if on a quest for the Holy Grail. The secular theology of nothingness is in conflict with itself. Ever since Darwin published *On the Origin of Species*, we learn that all living things are intrinsically equal. We're no longer "suspended above nature" as if by some metaphysical "skyhook," as the militantly secular philosopher Daniel Dennett puts it. We are nature herself, at her worst. And yet scientists strive to find signs of life elsewhere, life that presumably would be as ultimately insignificant as our own.

Dennett, an American philosopher, writer and cognitive scientist, is an evangelist for human-primate demotion. His books include such blunt instruments as *Breaking the Spell: Religion as a Natural Phenomenon* and *Darwin's Dangerous Idea: Evolution and the Meanings of Life,* in which he describes Darwin's theory of evolution by natural selection as a universal acid that eats through every theory of human behavior and every human achievement, particularly religion. Along with Richard Dawkins, Sam Harris and Christopher Hitchens, Dennett spearheaded the so-called New Atheist movement in which science both replaces and debunks faith. Religion's chief sin, they argue, lies in elevating humankind above the pond scum from whence we came. Their human-primate-put-down is not original. As noted, Duchamp got there first and did it better. More recently in Martin Amis's 1995 novel *The Information,* a character plans to write a book called *The History of Increasing Humiliation.* The title captures what Dennett and company have spent their lives doing: exuberantly, successfully and lucratively prosecuting the demotion of humankind, as if they were members of some sort of highly advanced tribe of latter day Aztec priests bent on cutting the spiritual heart out of every other living human until only their tribe of sceptics remain. Okay, that's an overstatement but, at the very least, they remind me of my missionary parents.

These days even the Wikipedia entry on evolutionary psychology traces our fall. It says that the action of natural selection upon "memes" (units of cultural transmission, the cultural equivalents of genes) undergoes selection and recombination.

Even our beliefs are understood to be rooted in our genetic evolution, not in what we have assumed was our free choice to believe something or not.

Now it seems we can't even lord it over our vegetable patches! The line between plants and animals has been blurred. At the very moment evolutionary psychologists debunked our capacity for free will and showed our brains to be self-deluding, other scientists elevated the non-brained as our equals. Neurobiologists are redefining the word *intelligence* as the ability to respond adaptively. We find ourselves side-by-side with cherry tomatoes as equally cognizant citizens of the universe. As Dennett said in a *New Yorker* article "How Smart Are Plants?" (December 23, 2013) on the intelligence of florae, "The idea that there is a bright line, with real comprehension and real minds on the far side of the chasm, and animals or plants on the other—that's an archaic myth."

I have a nagging question though: if we're nothing, why bother to convince us of our nothingness? Who cares? I would like to have asked Sagan why he bothered to write with such poetic skill and beauty about the meaninglessness of writing, given our transitory and diminutive place in the universe.

As Sagan wasn't available, later in the day that began with stargazing and peeing on my lawn, I set aside my cosmological questions and mowed the grass. I was happy even though I hate mowing. It's hot, noisy, polluting, and uncomfortable and I only do it to keep the mosquitoes down so my grandchildren have a pleasant place to play. Nevertheless, on that blistering, late July afternoon, while straddling the riding mower, being attacked by greenhead flies, wearing ear protectors to muffle the sound of the engine, and breathing the exhaust, I experienced intense pleasure. As I drove the mower, I reached out and snagged one of the first sun-warmed, ripe tomatoes of the season, chomped down on a luxuriant mouthful and fell through time into what I'll call the Eternal Present.

XV

It was Camilla Tilling's fault. Just before mowing I'd gotten an email from her, along with photographs attached. The sunny pictures were of herself, her husband, and their children sitting on "my" beach! Camilla had gone to the hotel I recommended and was there *at that very moment.* She'd unintentionally stirred such poignant memories of the happiest days of my childhood that I had an ache in my chest. And that was even *before* snagging a sun-warmed tomato!

The taste of fresh, warm tomato evoked a powerful rush of childhood memory. It tasted *exactly* like the tomatoes I ate more than fifty years ago while on vacation with my parents near Portofino, Italy. The owner of the small *pensione* where we stayed in Paraggi—a five-house hamlet a twenty-minute walk from Portofino overlooking the only sandy beach in the area—had a kitchen garden. She picked tomatoes, peppers, eggplants and zucchini just before she cooked and served them to us each day. So with one bite into the dusky, luscious flesh I was no longer in New England but transported to the Italy of my golden child-hood memories. As the wind direction changed, the stink of riding mower exhaust gave way to the sweet, muddy scent of the tidal flats beyond the marsh. The late afternoon sunlight cast the trees and tall marsh grass into backlit perfection. Not for the first time I thought that this gorgeous universe would be such a waste if it were unobserved and unremembered.

Aren't we lucky that we're storytellers? Isn't the universe lucky to have us! Isn't Bach lucky to have Camilla, standing in the middle of an orchestra while singing his St. Matthew Passion, while sensing Bach's spirit coursing through her, and perhaps God's spirit, too?

Later that afternoon, I prepared chicken stock because while on family vacation, we'd often eat *pastina in brodo* with tomato salads drizzled with olive oil and salt. Camilla's email and that tomato had inspired me to jump headlong into recreating one of the meals I love to remember. I turned on the radio while I unwrapped a chicken and peeled onions, carrots and garlic cloves and dropped them into a stockpot. Two scientists being interviewed on the NPR program *Science Friday* were speculating that life on Earth might have started on Mars, traveled here in a meteorite as a frozen organism and then evolved into complex life forms. Although Mars may once have had "better conditions for life to begin than Earth did, perhaps Earth was a better place for it to have evolved fully."

One speculated, "Maybe it took two planets to get life started." The other said, "I mean, how many times would there be two planets with the right conditions in the right place at the right time the right distance from each other like that?" Then he called the two-planets-plus-a-meteorite theory "pessimistic." Then they talked about the idea that a more "optimistic" theory of life's origin would be one that increased the odds of life beginning here and elsewhere rather than decreasing the chances by adding two-planets-plus-a-meteorite complexity to an already statistically improbable occurrence.

What I found even more interesting than the scientists' speculations about life's origins was otherwise dispassionate scientists using value-laden words like *pessimistic* and *optimistic* when rating the odds of whether or not we're alone in the universe.

I get it. I want there to be something more out there, too. After all, solitary confinement drives prisoners mad and most primates become anxious, angry and prone to hallucinations. That's because shared experiences are at the heart of what makes life worth living. Ayn Rand aside, much as we like to think of ourselves as isolated nomads bumping up against each other from time to time, we *are* our relationships, hence my preparing *pastina in brodo* and tomato salad through which I wanted to share my memories with my wife, and all because Camilla sent me a picture and I ate a tomato!

—

If according to Sagan and company I'm a microbe on a blue dot, what's the point of telling Genie about snagging a sun-warmed tomato that evoked the sweet taste of childhood? What's the point of Camilla taking her children on vacation and sending me a picture? What's the point of trying to carry Genie with me into my Eternal Present through cooking small pastas in chicken broth and serving the result with a generous grating of the best Parmesan cheese? The *point* is that I live as if my experiences are meaningful, notwithstanding religious and secular theologies of human insignificance. I feel significant when I tell my stories, therefore I am.

XVI

Scientists and theologians can't offer better than circular arguments, because there are no other kinds of arguments. Bible believers quote the Bible, and scientists quote other scientists. How do either scientists or theologians answer this question about the accuracy of their conclusions: "In reference to what?"

Our status as fallen sinners or diminished and newly humbled microbes is calculated in reference to biblical or scientific stories that are self-reinforcing. Is there a frame of reference relative to which we can define not just the motion of all things but also our experience of reality, even our meaning?

Maybe there is… sort of.

In 1989, the COBE satellite went into orbit around Earth to measure the radiation echo of the birth of our universe, an event astronomer Fred Hoyle dubbed the Big Bang—a snub that turned out to be descriptively true. We call this radiation echo cosmic microwave background radiation (CBR). Because CBR permeates space we can use it as our "compared-to-what" frame of reference. Spaceship Earth is moving—with respect to the CBR—at a speed we describe as 390 kilometers per second. We can also specify the so-called direction of our journey.

Next time you're peeing on your lawn and look into the night sky, try to spot the constellation Leo. We're moving toward

Leo at 390 kilometers per second. Of course, the words "390 kilometers per second" are just metaphors, just another poetic story to describe our experience of reality, not the thing itself. For all the intrinsic meaning of the word *kilometer*, we might just as well say that "we're moving toward Leo at three pizzas and a cabbage per walrus."

Whatever else I know, the actual experience of looking up into the night sky transcends descriptions in the same way that hearing Camilla sing is an entirely different experience than reading about her. And light isn't any faster or slower than the surge of delight I experience as Lucy and Jack listen to me describe what it was like to awake on the much anticipated morning of the first day of our vacation.

What's bigger, my memory, as I send it to Jack and Lucy brain-to-brain one story at a time, or the Great Attractor? What is stronger, the rush of emotion I feel hearing the opening notes of Beethoven's Fourth Piano Concerto, as I tell Jack and Lucy how I remember sitting with my mother as we listened to this music, or the force of the Great Attractor mysteriously pulling us to points unknown?

I refuse to be intimidated by theologians or scientists with their arbitrary scales of size, time and meaning. Genie bestows my meaning by listening. So do Lucy and Jack. So did Camilla as she listened to me telling her about my mother during a long flight.

Science can't predict what stories my children's great grandchildren will tell. The ultimate story about the experience of our journey into consciousness is a closed book to theologians and scientists alike, but it is not a book without promise. At this point we've barely cracked the introduction, and already smartass scientists and theologians pretend they know not just how the story started but how it ends—and worse—what it means or doesn't mean.

———

Someday I'll show the movie *Seabiscuit* to Jack and Lucy. On November 1, 1938, President Roosevelt and 40 million other people listening to the radio were captivated by a match race at the Pimlico Race Course between Seabiscuit, the underdog, and War Admiral. Seabiscuit was a small, insignificant horse, "the horse from the other side of the tracks who became a champion," wrote one commentator. In the movie, a reporter reacting to the coast-to-coast publicity for the race expresses doubt at Seabiscuit's chances: "That's an awful lotta hoopla for such a little horse."

To which Seabiscuit's jockey, Red Pollard, responds, "Though he be but little, he is fierce."

"What's that?" asks the reporter.

"That's Shakespeare, boys, Shakespeare," says Red.

Red's response nicely captures the folly of assessing meaning by anything other than poetry. And poetry is only spirit rather than material, love in action, love of life, love of words, love of beauty, even love of beautifully expressed ugliness. Poetry is play, more like a child's game than "serious." Therefore it is the most serious form of expression of all for the same reason that, until they grow up, children are transparent.

Red knew calculations of scale and meaning and size and strength must include matters of the spirit. So did Laura Hillenbrand, the unlikely author of the fabulous book upon which the movie is based.

Hillenbrand (a hero of mine) was forced to leave college before graduation when she contracted chronic fatigue syndrome, with which she has struggled ever since. She can barely leave her house. She suffers when she writes and it takes an enormous act of the will for her to do the most ordinary things. Yet, Hillenbrand wrote a classic that, at least temporarily, liberates me from mortality. Hillenbrand is an example of what Jesus was talking about: the truth of *being* is not found in the outer trappings, but in the spirit. Hillenbrand, Jesus, Seabiscuit—all unlikely cornerstones rejected by society, all reaching to the heart of the matter, all suffering and also triumphing—all changing my perception.

On the irony of writing about physical limits while being so incapacitated herself, Hillenbrand, says, "I'm looking for a way out of here. I can't have it physically, so I'm going to have it intellectually. It was a beautiful thing to ride Seabiscuit in my imagination" (*Washington Post*, November 28, 2010). Put another way, what is truer than a story about a journey into one person's Eternal Present powered by a single bite of tomato on a summer afternoon? In that moment, I vividly re-experienced being eight years old and sitting on a terrace overlooking the Mediterranean Sea while eating lunch with my parents. Saying that my ability to encode and retrieve personal experiences, called episodic memory, is supported by the circuitry of my medial temporal lobe, is just another way to say that sometimes the taste of a fresh tomato brings tears to my eyes. It reminds me of the times my beautiful young mother handed me a ripe slice and said "Taste *this* darling!" She's gone but her love abides. And that love can be triggered and made alive by the sacrament of gardening and storytelling or even getting an emailed picture from an opera singer who was a stranger—until she wasn't.

Saying that plants have a "level of intelligence that rivals ours" may be true, but do they pine for lost childhoods? Do they tell stories about experiencing life as a beautiful narrative? Do tears fall as they take a first bite of a plant they grew with their grandchild because they know how much their mother would have loved the moment? Does the color contrast of the fruit to the vine make them want to paint a picture? When it's 4 a.m., and they are sick of writing, do they find inspiration in a writer who got the job done through a veil of tears and say to themselves, "Laura Hillenbrand did it, so just quit whining and write!"

I tell my grandchildren about what it was like to throw open the shutters on the first morning of our summer vacation while knowing that the entire holiday lay ahead of me. I tell Amanda and Ben and Lucy and Jack how I ran out of the pensione to be the first person on the beach each year. I tell them about watching the sun rising over a turquoise sea and how deliciously cold the wet sand felt under my feet. I tell them about how the taste of a fresh-picked tomato reconnects me to that time and place and to my darling mother. And as I hand Lucy a tomato just plucked from a vine she helped plant, her eyes sparkle as brightly as that far off sea. My grandchild will remember this moment. And that is no small thing.

XVII

Some of my friends like Sam don't get why I "still" go to church. When they say, "Frank, God's only in your head!" my answer is, "Yeah, whatever. What isn't?"

Or as the poet Yehuda Amichai writes in Gods Come and Go, Prayers Remain Forever:

> *I say with perfect faith*
> *that prayers precede God.*
> *Prayers created God.*
> *God created man,*
> *And man creates prayers*
> *that create God who creates man.*

My question isn't, "Did I create God who creates me?" but, "Do I need God, however he, she or it came to be?" My question isn't "Can I find a church, mosque, synagogue, a gathering of atheists or some other temple that's perfect to stroke me?" but "Where can I find spiritual beauty that feeds my soul?"

I've been lucky. My experience of going to a small Greek Orthodox church has been good. I found myself in a community that is welcoming. I say "lucky" because Genie's and my experience is not always the norm. The last thing I'm doing here is trying to get anyone to convert to anything.

I've been going to the same church for twenty-five years and can tell you that although our denomination is full of problems, I still love to attend, at least most of the time. I choose to go not because I think I'm closer to the truth in church, but because of my very personal religion-infested background.

Put it this way: church may be a son-of-a-bitch, but it's *my* son-of-a-bitch! I also choose to try my best to be honest about problems in the church of my choice. Jesus did that too. He criticized everything religious around him yet still participated in the traditional liturgical formal worship of his day even though it was led by hypocrites he denounced.

In the Greek Orthodox Church women can't serve at the altar, let alone be priests or bishops. A woman may "eat Jesus' flesh" and "drink his blood," but, heaven forfend, she may *not* walk into the altar area reserved for males only and dust the icons or the sky will fall! And if she's in a North American Orthodox community she is more than likely to find herself in some sort of Hellenistic or Russian or Arab ethnic club. Her local congregation may well include converts from rightwing evangelical churches bent on making the Orthodox as intolerant and hell-bent as themselves.

She also risks being coerced into spiritual bondage by perverts acting the part of holy men and women who like to be in control of others. There are some Orthodox priests and monks who brilliantly play the part of holy men. They use long beards and quiet voices as props while seeking to control gullible people by demanding that they become their "spiritual children." Some Orthodox seeking certainty and direction latch on to these gurus. (The phenomena of some religious leaders trying to control people through religion is not unknown in Protestant and Roman Catholic circles either.) This allows a few power-hungry priests, monks and nuns who are no more than high functioning sociopaths claiming to speak for God, to sniff around every area of their followers' lives, especially their sex lives.

Over the years, I've had good experiences with the priests in my local church and have also enjoyed some wonderful times of retreat in several great Orthodox monastic communities. That said, my presence in our lovely local church could be construed as a kind of condoning of my not-so-lovely denomination's overall problems. We're sexist, we're nationalistic and there are fundamentalist manipulators in our midst! And I go to a local church that belongs to a denomination like *that*! Shame on me!

Then again, if I only wanted to attend a church that was good, true and without error—according to my transitory ego-stoked beliefs—I'd have to invent my own religion. But wait a moment. There'd be a problem. I'd have to excommunicate the priest and his entire congregation! You see, I know that particular bishop/priest/congregation too well. With apologies to Groucho Marx: I'd never want to join a church that had someone like me for their founding bishop, especially if I was the *only* member!

I go to church as my means of trying to encounter God, not as a way to look for perfection on earth. I don't go because I think my church is a better church, let alone the one true church. It's just where I go. It's just my means of establishing relationships with people who share my commitment to a liturgical tradition that I am fed by aesthetically and spiritually. Or put it this way: the Dude abides.

In the movie *The Big Lebowski*, the Dude Lebowski (a single, unemployed slacker living in Venice, California) is mistaken for a millionaire who is also named *Lebowski*. Thugs break into the Dude's apartment and try to coerce him into paying a debt he knows nothing about. When he refuses, they pee on his carpet. Later, while considering the immorality of the self-identified

Nihilists who desecrated the Dude's carpet, his friend Walter says, "Nihilists! Fuck me. I mean, say what you want about the tenets of National Socialism, Dude, at least it's an ethos."

Unlike the nihilist carpet wreckers, Walter (played by John Goodman) and the Dude (played by Jeff Bridges) do have an ethos! They embrace this code by bowling. To them, bowling is church, their means of establishing relationships with people who share their commitment to a liturgical tradition in a way that centers their lives. And their church isn't perfect either but they still go, even though it also includes jerks, like "Jesus Quintana" played by John Turturro. Turturro's hilarious "Jesus" is a pain in the ass, notwithstanding Walter and the Dude still go bowling with him. They don't see themselves as too good for whoever else shows up to participate.

The Dude is into liturgical tradition. He practices his rituals religiously, which include smoking marijuana in the bath, drinking White Russians, bowling and remaining faithful to his friends. The Dude *abides*, because he's true to his rites and thus, to himself. The Dude does not worry about his motivations, let alone his inner sincerity or the perfection of his bowling-church. The Dude is not trying to change his liturgical rites to make them hipper, progressive or modern. The Dude isn't a bowler because he believes in bowling but because he bowls!

My life is also shaped by liturgical rites: praying as I walk down the stairs, bringing a cup of coffee to Genie in bed, telling my grandchildren stories, drinking wine with Genie before and during dinner, writing each day before dawn, reading the *New Yorker* before bed, and having sex with Genie as we push back against mortality's grasp—while also fulfilling our appetites. *And* then there's church.

Like the Dude, "or His Dudeness, or Duder or El Duderino, if you're not into the whole brevity thing," the ancient Byzantine liturgies abide. Speaking *only for myself,* the Liturgy provides the interior space I crave, wherein I may "lay aside all earthly cares," as the words of the prayer during the Great Entrance instruct.

The Great Entrance is a procession during which the clergy enter the sanctuary through the Holy Doors that lead to the altar. The priest, altar boys (where are the altar girls?) and deacons carry incense and candles, and the angels are said to enter with them. During these rituals, I'm not listening to a sermon or trying to decide if some preacher or other is clever or if I agree with him, let alone wondering if I believe in the angels the choir is singing about. The Liturgy isn't about being taught, any more than music is about doing math. As Jesus said, it's all about the spirit, not the geography. Liturgy is about providing a silent space inside me where words are replaced by an experience of another dimension where I may sense the love of God.

What I'm "looking for" in church is inner stillness and peace of the kind my friend Holly Meade lived out as she faced her death, not an adrenaline rush or entertainment, let alone spectacle. I do not need more entertainment! I live in a time and place where I'm bombarded by entertainment 24/7. Nor do I need more celebrity leaders or Bible teachers. I'm not looking for clever new words about so-called theological facts but for the experience of spirituality itself. The last thing I crave is to be exposed to the sort of grandstanding preachers that so many evangelical churches seem to breed with the ubiquity of maggots appearing in road kill. The last thing I want is a new and improved "worship experience." The last thing I want is for the service to be socially and politically relevant or, worse yet, politicized, as if faith is about who I should vote for according to a moralistic left wing *or* right wing litmus test. I just want to go bowling!

I no more want my liturgies updated than I want the house I live in knocked down so I can build a better, different or bigger house. What would happen to Lucy's stair on which I always pray for her? What would happen to the inside of the kitchen dish cupboard where the heights and measurements of my children and grandchildren are marked? What would become of the cabinet door that's dented from the time Genie threw a salad bowl at me? What would happen to the loose, squeaky floorboard where I knelt the time I asked my daughter Jessica to forgive me for slapping her when she was a child, and where she forgave me?

XVIII

My way of trying to encounter God within a church community may well be poison for others. We all bring our backgrounds with us. We're all running from something. For instance, I know several people raised in the Orthodox Church who have fled to evangelical communities and found God there, or at least found a happier version of themselves. I know other people who share my sort of religious background and they can only find spiritual solace in gatherings of atheists. More power to them! We are all recovering from what we've experienced in captivity to ourselves.

———

When I first joined the Greek Orthodox Church in 1990 I argued the finer points of theology and church history with my long-suffering evangelical mother and sisters. (Dad was spared, having died in 1984.) I argued as if any church I happened to join was ipso-facto the gatekeeper to heaven. I argued in a way that implied that a human could find THE TRUTH and judge others by it. I argued in a way that denied that our brains process what we hear and see and touch and, therefore, all information is just another story. I even wrote a book (*Dancing Alone*) about all that is theologically and historically wrong with the Protestant Reformed tradition I'd fled. I laced my book with the zealous spirit of proselytizing certainty typical of the fundamentalist born-again religion I thought I'd escaped.

Eventually, I had to admit that I didn't join the Orthodox Church for theological or even religious reasons. I joined it for a psychological reason. My new church wasn't my childhood faith and I needed a change.

When I began to go to an Orthodox church, I wanted to find a way to escape my past, my culture and myself. Eventually, I came to see that a little honesty is in order. First off, I hadn't *become* anything. I hadn't gotten "saved." The Orthodox view of salvation is that it's not a series of magical steps, akin to the one-time born-again experience, but a journey. According to the Orthodox tradition, a person never becomes saved, because we are always *becoming*.

To the extent I was becoming Orthodox, it was mostly for aesthetic reasons. I couldn't stand the American evangelical experience any longer for the same sort of reasons that I prefer swimming in the ocean to a swimming pool.

Where we go to church, or whether we go, isn't the point. The point is who are we *becoming*? Does church help you to become the sort of person you'd pick to be stuck on a desert island with? Good! Go! Does it hurt your chances of becoming that person? Run!

Flee from exclusionary certainty. As the bumper sticker says, "Mean People Suck!" And that goes especially for people who are mean in the name of love.

There is only one defense against the rising, worldwide, fear-filled fundamentalist tide engulfing all religions (including the intolerant religion of the New Atheists) which once engulfed me: the embrace of paradox and uncertainty as the virtuoso expression of love.

The follower of Jesus' example—be she an atheist scientist working on a neuropsychology project, a pastor counseling gang members, a husband bringing his wife her coffee or a mom picking up her child at preschool—will do anything it takes to live the reality of what it means to walk in another person's shoes. To help us do *that* is the only point of going to any church or, for that matter, logging on to an atheist website.

Atheists, believers, and everyone in between can show empathy equally well. It never is about correct belief, but is always about character. And religious people and atheists are no better or worse than each other.

If you are a Church Of One, do you trust your congregation? When you want to be inspired by an icon representing something bigger than yourself, don't you ever get tired of just looking into the mirror?

We're all stuck in the same rudderless boat. It is about the spirit we share or about nothing. It is about how we treat others or about nothing. How we treat others is the only proof of truth we have. That proof is not found in any book. It is only found in the expression of unconditional trust we may sometimes see in the eyes of the people who know us best.

XIX

Genie once said to me, "It's hard to believe in something that seems too good to be true." Then she thought about it for a moment and added, "But sometimes good things *are* true, even things that are too good to believe."

In an essay titled, "When the Other Appears on the Scene," philosopher, literary critic and novelist Umberto Eco muses on what I think of as Genie's theme of hopeful uncertainty. He writes:

> To accept even if only for a moment the idea that there is no God; that man appeared in the world out of a blunder on the part of maladroit fate, delivered not only unto his mortal condition but also condemned to be aware of this, and for this reason the most imperfect of all creatures … in order to find the courage to await death, we would necessarily become a religious animal, and would aspire to the construction of narratives capable of providing us with an explanation and a model, an exemplary image. And among the many stories we imagine—some dazzling, some awe-inspiring, some pathetically comforting—in the fullness of time we have at a certain point the religious, moral, and poetic strength to conceive the model of Christ, of universal love, of forgiveness for enemies, of

a life sacrificed that others may be saved. If I were a traveler from a distant galaxy and I found myself confronted with a species capable of proposing this model, I would be filled with admiration... I would judge this wretched and vile species, which has committed so many horrors, redeemed were it only for the fact that it has managed to wish and to believe that all this is the truth... [T]he fact that this story could have been imagined and desired by humans, creatures who know only that they do not know, would be just as miraculous (miraculously mysterious) as the son of a real God being made flesh. This natural and worldly mystery would not cease to move and ennoble the hearts of those who do not believe.

—

I glimpse the *beauty*, the *love* and the *peace* that is—as Genie puts it so wonderfully—too good to be true during an annual service we treasure, the Service of Forgiveness. This is a service only a liturgical community could provide. After prayers the service ends with each person in our local church walking to the front of the sanctuary, kissing the icon of Jesus and then bowing in front of our priest. "Forgive me," we say. "I forgive you," answers our priest. We embrace and then we say, "God forgives us both." Each person then takes his or her place next to the priest in a line that eventually stretches around the interior of our church.

Each person repeats the action and moves down the line repeating the "Forgive me" ritual with everyone until we've each asked one another for forgiveness and have all been forgiven. We bow before children and old people, middle-aged parishioners and giggling toddlers. We ask forgiveness from people we love and from people we don't love and even from some we dislike. The priest and the youngest infant in arms are equals in this ritual.

When I get to Genie, I whisper "Forgive me." We hug as we've hugged others, but in Genie's embrace I tumble into a healing moment of sweet reconciliation. My wife says, "I forgive you," with deep warmth and sincerity. And she really knows me! Yet, I am forgiven! I realize that life is not a step to a better place: life IS the better place, right here and now. It's too good to be true—and it's real.

XX

I have no idea why, but by the time she was four years old, Lucy loved Greek mythology. I read her some stories out of a young reader's Greek mythology book meant for "ages 12 and up." Lucy listened for hours. Then she revisited the stories in our conversations and weighed them up. "This isn't real," was a standard comment of hers, usually uttered after I'd been reading some long episode involving murder, the creation of mythical beings and bad endings for assorted mortals who had run afoul of the gods.

Lucy's doubts about the Greek myths began to bleed into her interpretation of Bible stories. After we moved from reading a toddler Bible to a young adult illustrated Bible when Lucy was four, she began to weigh each story in a new way. I let her decide for herself which stories received the "This is real" or "This isn't real" verdict.

When we read about Jonah, Lucy announced, "Jonah isn't real, Ba. It's just a story like Persephone eating the food of the dead." When I once claimed Goldilocks had come into our house one morning and stolen all our breakfast cereal, Lucy knowingly observed, "Goldilocks *isn't* real, Ba!"

On the other hand, Lucy felt most of the stories about Jesus were real. Did he raise Lazarus from the dead? "Yes, Ba, this actually happened." I listened expectantly. "He made Mary and Martha so happy!" she exclaimed.

When we read Bible stories and Greek mythology, Lucy's skepticism was contagious. I hadn't spent much time with the Bible for some time. Since leaving the evangelical fold (and the overdose of Bible I ingested there), I only dipped in once in a while looking for references. My explorations with Lucy and Jack were like revisiting a house I'd lived in long ago. I found it smaller than I remembered. Universal floods, falls from grace, demons, devils, people going down into the underworld after death, sinners suffering torment, saviors, resurrections and heavenly battles swirl through Greek mythology and biblical stories alike. Re-encountering these Bible stories afresh through Lucy's and Jack's eyes was like coming home for the summer holidays after being at boarding school in England when I was ten and discovering that my old bedroom seemed so much smaller than I remembered it.

If there were no "holy books" how much easier it would be to believe in God! An oral tradition and a rich liturgical expression of divinity lovingly shared in a faith community are much more convincing than words on a page. The images I see from the Hubble telescope do more to suggest a loving creative God besotted by beauty than most Bible passages. One hug from Amanda, Ben, Lucy or Jack teaches me more about the mystery of unconditional love being the animating spirit of the universe than most Bible passages ever could.

Consider the gospel of Luke. There are timeless passages in Luke chapter 6 offering a reason to hope that Jesus is the best path to a better future. Sadly, those enlightened passages are the exception. Most of the Bible is so time-bound and culturally limited that it defeats faith rather than building it. Yet Luke 6 is the foundation of just about every good thing that has come from Jesus to us.

Try to read this passage as it might have been heard in a world where torture was legal, women taken in adultery were stoned to death, an eye-for-an-eye was the norm, *and* religion was so rigid and codified that people spent lifetimes ritually purifying themselves over normal bodily functions. Hear the words as if you never read them.

> Blessed be you poor: for yours is the kingdom of God.
>
> Blessed are you that hunger now: for you shall be filled.
>
> Blessed are you that weep now: for you shall laugh.
>
> Blessed are you, when men shall hate you, and when they shall separate you from their company, and shall reproach you, and cast out your name as evil, for the Son of man's sake.
>
> Rejoice in that day, and leap for joy: for, behold, your reward is great in heaven: for in the like manner did their fathers to the prophets.
>
> But woe unto you that are rich for you have received your consolation.
>
> Woe to you that are full for you shall hunger.
>
> Woe to you that laugh now for you shall mourn and weep.
>
> Woe to you, when all men shall speak well of you for so did their fathers to the false prophets.
>
> But I say to you which hear, Love your enemies, and do good to them which hate you, bless them that curse you, and pray for them which despitefully use you.
>
> And to him that strikes you on the one cheek offer also the other; and him that takes away your cloak forbid not to take your coat also.

Give to every man that asks of you; and of him that takes away your goods ask them not again.

And as you would that men should do to you, do you also to them likewise.

For if you love them which love you, what thank have you for sinners also love those that love them.

And if you do well to them which do good to you, what thank have you for sinners also do even the same.

And if you lend to them of whom you hope to receive, what thank have you for sinners also lend to sinners, to receive as much again.

But love you your enemies, and do good, and lend, hoping for nothing again; and your reward shall be great, and you shall be the children of the Highest: for he is kind to the unthankful and to the evil.

Be you therefore merciful, as your Father also is merciful. Judge not, and you shall not be judged: condemn not, and you shall not be condemned: forgive, and you shall be forgiven: Give, and it shall be given to you; good measure, pressed down, and shaken together, and running over, shall men give into your bosom.

For with the same measure that you mete withal it shall be measured to you again.

If *only* the rest of the gospels were *consistent* with this passage. If *only* all the vengeful contradictory ranting about hell fire and judgment (that could *not* have been spoken by the same person we discover in Luke 6) hadn't been added. I say "added" because the hellfire passages represent the absolute contradiction of what you just read.

Forget theology. I'm writing here as a working author making a best guess. As a writer I know when the voice of a character shifts. That's one reason I quit the movie business and decided to write novels. The scripts I was hired to direct kept getting messed up by too many writers. I know an interloping paragraph when I run into it! Was the material added by writers and editors of the New Testament, threatening hell and so forth, put there when trying to scare people into their new church? Were the writers trying to win fights with the Jews who hadn't joined their new Jewish/Christian sect?

Jesus either said God "is kind to the unthankful and to the evil" or he said that God will burn his, her or its enemies in hell. You can't have it both ways.

So is *this* Jesus?

"Woe to you, Chorazin! Woe to you, Bethsaida! For if the miracles that were performed in you had been performed in Tyre and Sidon, they would have repented long ago, sitting in sackcloth and ashes. But it will be more bearable for Tyre and Sidon at the judgment than for you. And you, Capernaum, will you be lifted to the heavens? No, you will go down to Hades..."

...or is this Jesus?

"Be you therefore merciful, as your Father also is merciful. Judge not, and you shall not be judged: condemn not, and you shall not be condemned: forgive, and you shall be forgiven."

XXI

I'm compelled to offer thanks even though I understand less with every passing year. My knowledge diminishes as my gratitude grows.

On Holy Friday Lucy was in church decorating the wood "tomb" that houses the Epitaphios (the cloth icon of the dead Christ) with flowers. This elaborately carved wooden structure is about the size of a big freezer and looks like an open box on legs with a carved-wood canopy over it. The tomb is the central "actor" in our Holy Friday procession to commemorate Jesus' death. After the tomb is decorated with flowers, the Epitaphios is placed inside and carried in a procession through the streets with the entire congregation following it.

After working with a dozen women for several hours covering the tomb with flowers, Lucy exclaimed, "I'm going to do this every year, every year forever!"

"Every year forever" nicely captures the meaning of the word *abide*. Children love repeated experiences that give them a sense of mastery. As she pressed flowers into the wire mesh covering the ornately carved tomb, Lucy at age four intuitively grasped the value of tradition. She worked joyfully alongside the older women, imitating and mastering the art of sticking flower stems into wire mesh. She participated equally in the reenactment of preparing Christ for burial. *Doing* and *being* was a small girl's door into a joyful shared ritual. No one participating had invented this ritual, so they shared it and passed it on without possessive ego marring the experience. No one took the credit. Like some sort of spiritual national park the ritual was there to be enjoyed, cared for, and then, passed on.

The philosopher René Girard would have understood Lucy's joy in decorating Christ's tomb. She was in fellowship with a roomful of older women, enacting an ineffable mystery. In turn, alongside a child, they became as happily childlike as she. Lucy belonged! And while the suffering Christ was remembered, the bitter theology of retribution and atonement (in which God is said to have insisted someone should pay for all our sins) did not intrude.

Girard points to a non-retributive, non-theological understanding of Christ. He attempts to explain how religions, including certain branches of Christianity, have become so fixated on retributive sacrifice. He argues that human primates imitate one another, as all primates do, giving rise to violence. Because we imitate others, we imitate their desires. Through this "mimetic desire" (think miming), we begin to want what others want until we'll kill to get it. Such violence threatens survival of the tribe.

Girard argues that the problem of human violence was once solved with a "lesser" violence when people united against a communal scapegoat, allowing them to blame one person for whatever harm was befalling them. Former enemies united in hating the person they killed. Ritualized scapegoating became the foundation of religion. Girard argues that our mythologies describe what's *always* happening, not what happened once upon a time. So the Bible brought a transition from the scapegoat norm to something better.

Where pre-biblical myths were part of the dynamic of the scapegoat/vengeful/religion/sacrifice mechanism, the Bible contains some stories recounting the ethical evolution story *from the perspective of the victims.* Rather than always sanctioning the death of the scapegoat, even the Old Testament God is sometimes on the side of the victim. Girard implies that the theological idea of so-called atonement—a euphemism for the appeasement of an angry God—is wrong.

The idea of atonement—Jesus "dying for our sins" as if to satisfy God—is the opposite of evolutionary truth. Evolution doesn't demand justice; it demands *life.* In evolution the result of suffering, killing, extinctions, death and chaos is the learning curve undertaken by genes that pass on knowledge in an effort to *survive.* No one from the first primitive microorganism to Jesus has died to "satisfy" an angry God.

If there is a Creator by whatever name, then our very existence puts that Creator on the side of *life.* The evolutionary method is not about changes in life forms bent on dying. Why would the Creator be the enemy of his, her, or its own creation and anything or anyone in it, including a divine son? Nature may be many things but it is not petty, vindictive and stupid. So why should we think God is?

Can you imagine me consigning Lucy to oblivion because she had wrong ideas about me? Can you imagine me burning her forever because she didn't believe in me, forgot my name, called me the wrong name, thought I had six arms, believed she had three or six or ten grandfathers, or brought me fruit when I'd asked for lamb? And even if a grandchild killed me and I could judge her or him from the grave, do you imagine that I'd demand they burn for eternity? I am not a good man and yet can you imagine *anything* that would cut Amanda, Ben, Lucy and Jack off from my love?

Following Girard's argument, death—including Jesus' death—occurs so that all may live, learn and eventually reach an end point of perfection when the entire cycle of creation from the beginning to end will be vindicated, perhaps even understood. A great milestone has already been passed on our evolutionary journey: consciousness has achieved empathy. Paradoxically, human society may be on an ethical journey but evolution as defined by science is only focused on survival, mirroring another paradox: although the Bible (supposedly) opposes persecution, Christianity has been complicit in the coercion of heretics, the killing of Jews, the persecution of gay men and women and the perpetuation of wars.

Girard argues that while the gospel is God's revelation, we understand its meaning only gradually. Girard credits the best non-retributive Christian and Jewish thinking for the humanism that is usually credited exclusively to secular thought. In the West, he notes, the move away from scapegoating is not the product of the Enlightenment but rather the result of the enlightened teaching of Jesus, (affirming my view that the Enlightenment was a Christian heresy). The scientific spirit, like the spirit of enterprise, was a *byproduct* of the action of the gospel as Girard says in *Things Hidden since the Foundation of the World.* He writes "I hold the truth is not an empty word, or a mere 'effect' as people say nowadays. I hold that everything capable of diverting us from madness and death, from now on, is inextricably linked with this truth." For Girard this truth is manifested in Jesus.

XXII

It was a bright September day, clear, cool and perfect. Genie, Lucy, Jack and my daughter-in-law, Becky, were sprawled on the lawn. Lucy wandered over to the vegetable garden and picked cherry tomatoes. She ate them while dancing and watching her shadow flicker over the grass. Becky was starting to show with her third child. Love, contentment and sweetness were as palpable as the sunlight.

The whole world pines for these sublime moments. We spend entire lifetimes striving to achieve fragments of peace. Tragedies when babies are killed or children are ripped from mothers, are tragic only because we compare the sorrow to the joy that might have been and to those glimpses of perfection that come our way. It is our fate to pine for what we lose. It is our fate to fear the loss of what we love.

There would be no Holocaust museums chronicling horror unless there was a sense that horror is abnormal and, therefore, preventable. Yet, if we insist on a material-universe-only view of ourselves, we have to admit that the story of evolution proves that suffering, death and extinction are inevitable. Yet, we impose a human ethical standard on the material world. This imposition is not fact-based if we insist on understanding that facts relate only to the material universe.

Most people don't really want to live only according to narrowly defined material facts. Most of us try to direct our human primate evolutionary process along ethical non-material lines. We impose standards that do not come from nature. Nature is cruel yet we try not to be. We prosecute people for war crimes that are no more destructive than what happens every day in the churning cauldron of life where everything is eaten and where death is the only incubator of life. We call murder wrong although it's the most natural thing on earth.

We've decided to let an imagined utopian ideal, a future Eden if you will, rule our present despite this being a spiritual non-material-universe-based choice that flies in the face of natural selection. We impose ethics that exist only in our heads upon the material universe. We are part of nature yet we have decided to be nicer than nature. There would be no war crimes trials unless our ethically evolved selves questioned the method of evolution itself. There would be no tears after the death of a friend like Holly, unless we had it in us to dream beyond what by now we should be used to.

A spiritual non-material-based way of life turns out to be the *actual* way we live no matter what we say we believe. We live by ethics not found in nature and we enrich our lives with art. That says something to me. Maybe a purely material view of the universe and of ourselves is not in fact a fact.

We have moments when we say to ourselves, "This is as good as it gets." When we use the word *good* it has as much intrinsic meaning to us as the words "two plus two equals four." Each of us may have a variation on what prompts us to say, "This is as good as it gets," but we all know what we mean by the phrase and what others mean.

If there were no spiritual side to us, there would be no sense of loss when the material universe intrudes on our happiness.

We'd just accept the evolutionary method. "Death leads to life— so quit complaining!" we'd say. I'd take no pleasure in being a kinder grandfather than I was a father. Holly Meade's death would not be a loss; it would just be the next thing that happened. I would not have been comforted by meeting Camilla as I flew home wrapped in my sorrow. In other words we are spiritual creatures in a material world.

In theology, transubstantiation is the doctrine that the substance of the bread and the wine used in the sacrament of the Eucharist is changed, not merely as by a sign or a figure, but also in reality. This magical alchemy is no less impossible to explain than the magical alchemy of transubstantiation that's performed when a scientist describes the gasses exploding to form a billion mile-long column of light as beautiful. This is transubstantiation, too. The physical world is changed into a spiritual fact. Jesus' words, "Man does not live by bread alone" are given a new depth. Photographs used to gather data become pieces of art. Millions more human primates derive a sense of meaning from the pictures' beauty than learn scientific facts from them.

The science is debated. Words like *dark matter*, are tossed around. These words are metaphors for actual things that are what they are without our explanations. When we declare these things beautiful, my hunch is that they were beautiful before we were around to observe them or invented language to express opinions about what we find ourselves looking at.

The creation of stars and their destruction were going on before we looked up and will continue long after the last person disappears. They exist. That's all. And for whatever reason, it seems to me that they are *intrinsically* beautiful. Beauty is real. The meaning of our existence was enriched when the first primate looked up and said "That is beautiful." Hubble's lasting legacy is art not science. And science is beautiful too. Science can extend lives but it can also illumine our spiritual nature. In his *History of Western Philosophy* Bertrand Russell wrote about the beauty of mathematical science: "Mathematics, rightly viewed, possesses not only truth, but supreme beauty—a beauty cold and austere, like that of sculpture, without appeal to any part of our weaker nature, without the gorgeous trappings of painting or music, yet sublimely pure, and capable of a stern perfection such as only the greatest art can show." Paul Erdős (one of the most prolific mathematicians of the twentieth century) said, "Why are numbers beautiful? It's like asking why Beethoven's Ninth Symphony is beautiful. If you don't see why, someone can't tell you. I know numbers are beautiful. If they aren't beautiful, nothing is."

Our longing for spiritual joy and our ability to appreciate beauty in a way that turns the physical world into a spiritual fact unnerves people who believe that spirituality is an illusion. They tend to demote notions of beauty along with demoting us. Like restaurant critics who hate food, some adamantly secular art critics have promoted art that denies the very *idea* of art. They have championed minimalist and absurdist art, theater, writing and music that closed more doors than they opened. These critics seemed to rejoice in the kind of artistic segregation that drew an ever tighter circle excluding all but the initiated.

Each meaning-busting work they endorsed left future writers, composers and artists with less to work with. How do you follow Duchamp's urinal hung on a wall? (Sherrie Levine has made several "re-appropriating" works of art. So now there's a gold-plated "Fountain after Marcel Duchamp" but you know what I mean...) Levine aside, what do you compose next after John Cage's *4'-33"* (four minutes, thirty-three seconds) of *silence?* I'd argue that you can compose such a statement piece just once to make the point, but starting a trend of nothingness is utterly absurd. How do you write a novel if you believe that narrative and storytelling are passé?

The humanities are about one thing: the soul. Declare the soul dead or mere brain chemistry and the humanities die. Declare culture nothing but a contest between men and women or all about politics or elites and you suck the life out of human aspiration.

The prejudice against art work that speaks of purpose and spiritual values, began after the mass slaughter of World War One. Value and purpose were attacked and so were craft and even the notion of beauty. Traditional ideas about meaning and religion were blamed for the insanity and hubris of nationalism and suicidal war within "Christendom."

In the forefront of shaping attitudes were some members of the Bloomsbury Group. The main group included writers, intellectuals, and philosophers like Virginia Woolf, E.M. Forster, John Maynard Keynes, Roger Fry, and Lytton Strachey. They shared a horrified reaction to the slaughter of the First World War, and turned their loss of faith and loss of confidence in the old values into a crusade for secular modernity.

This dismissal of spirituality as passé extended to art. Although some members of the group, like Woolf and Forrester, truly did seek meaning, others used biting satire and literary criticism to react against the "bourgeois conventions" that had, as they saw it, led to the millions of dead in the Great War. For instance, Roger Fry mocked John Singer Sargent's paintings. At a 1926 Sargent retrospective in London, Fry dismissed his works as: "Wonderful indeed, but most wonderful that this wonderful performance should ever have been confused with that of an artist."

Artists like Sargent were dismissed as not modern enough, thus foreshadowing what happened in the twentieth century, at least for a while, to painters like Wayne Thiebaud, one of the greatest twentieth and twenty-first century American artists. But Fry was mistaken. Sargent survived Fry. And today Thiebaud's critics, who once dismissed him as too realistic and painterly, and then mistook him for a Pop artist (!), are seen to be the small-minded ideologues they were. It's the dead end of the Bloomsbury group's cynicism (and the self-conscious "moderns") that seems dated and empty now. I'm guessing that the same fate awaits the work of the more doctrinaire of the New Atheist authors of the late twentieth and early twenty-first centuries. It seems to me that a spiritual sensibility is built into human nature. Formal religion may or may not disappear but art, love and a desire to find beauty will remain. And humans will still strive to live according to spiritual values found only in their own heads that are contrary to nature so to speak.

Art, like religion, is harder to kill off than the religiously dedicated secularists of the twentieth century imagined. Put it this way: the once fashionable Damien Hirst, with his rotting sharks and sheep in tanks of formaldehyde, and the always unfashionable Thomas Kinkade, with his schmaltzy seven dwarfs' cottages that seem to be ripped from the background cells of Disney's *Snow White*, deserved each other. Their garbage is destined for the same historic trash pile. They both made fortunes, but that is all they made. And in the case of Hirst that is literally true. He opened a factory production line to manufacture his minimalist/found object/absurdist works en masse for the super-rich, while personally disdaining hands-on art making.

As Camille Paglia points out in her magnificent book *Glittering Images*, a deliberately induced art illiteracy has been foisted on the public by the art community and "young people walk through museums with little-to-no sense of context." Art history is shunned in favor of "what's happening now," even at the college level. Many people nowadays view art as they view fast cuts in commercials, no more than derivatives of derivatives as devalued as the financial derivatives that led to the early twenty-first century market crash. Paglia (a self-describe atheist) writes that "a culture can only be dismantled once. Then something must be built or art falls silent." Irony about irony is a dead-end she says. Parody has led to "a narcissistic art form that could be mistaken for a prank."

XXIII

What had been important to my parents—art, music, and spirituality—were bred into me. And that is one reason why John Singer Sargent's *The Daughters of Edward Darley Boit* (1882) "belongs" to Genie and me. Sargent placed the four Boit girls in their parents' darkened Paris drawing room, subtly lit with mirrors and reflections. All four are wearing white pinafores. The girls' expressions aren't posed or stiff, happy or unhappy, smiling or unfriendly. Rather, they are the relaxed "Oh it's you" type of expressions children wear when casually acknowledging a trusted family member who's just walked in.

The youngest girl, just three, sits on the floor and looks directly at us while two of the older girls, ten and twelve-years-old, ignore us. One child, a tall slim eight-year-old, stands alone staring at us with her hands clasped behind her back. Framing the painting are two Japanese vases, and their bright white porcelain heightens the effect of the children's pinafores, each one proof of Sargent's mastery of depicting white cloth. The thickness of the paint bears his signature fast and generous brush strokes, and renders the play of light as creamy, seductive, and so very real. But this is no *trompe l'oeil*. The paint is used honestly *as* paint, gloriously slathered-on white *paint*.

The vases themselves now stand in the gallery on either side of the painting. They seem to have time-traveled out of the picture, so when I visit the painting I half expect other elements to appear too, maybe even the Boit daughters themselves, to saunter around the corner.

Before it was moved to the new Art of the Americas wing in the Museum of Fine Arts in Boston, Genie and I used to view the picture of the Boit daughters while sitting on a big round gray velvet sofa. It had a very comfortable upholstered column in the middle to lean back on. In those days, the painting was displayed in a small low-ceilinged room down on the first floor. We sometimes snoozed on that old couch. I'd wake up with a jolt and catch the youngest child in Sargent's group portrait staring at me from where she sits on the floor with her doll. Half awake, I'd feel embarrassed that the youngest Boit daughter had caught me sleeping, again. But the couch was irresistible and the perfect place to rest midway through a visit to the museum. So we'd take our trek to what Genie called "Sargent's little girls" after lunch and hope not too many other people had the same idea.

Years later, Lucy (age four) and I walked through the huge new American wing atrium with its fifty-foot ceiling and a cafeteria that occupies the center of the big open space. We took the elevators up to the second floor so we could go see our little girls in their swanky new home. As we pushed open the heavy glass doors and walked into the Sargent gallery Lucy said, "See, Ba, everything is the same and where it is supposed to be!" She ran to the painting and reconnected with the Boit children while I sat down and watched her from the new and less comfortable couch.

I was thankful that we'd arrived early enough to briefly have the painting to ourselves. My granddaughter stood for a while staring at the painting then shuffling backwards to me, all the while with her eyes on the art, she plunked down on my lap without even looking around assuming, correctly, that I would guide her to a safe landing. Viewing the picture with Lucy in my arms, I succumbed to the powerful spell cast by Sargent as never before. It was as if the artwork had kidnapped me along with the little girl I was holding, and pulled us into a secret world inside the canvas. Lucy and the girls were very alike, and being alone with them while holding her connected me to their childhood world as if the distance and time had melted away and we were all in that playroom together.

———

We all have our druthers in art. Like the church we choose to go to (or not go to) art isn't about "The Truth" but about what feeds us individually. I happen to love the art of the Italian Renaissance. On my personal planet I'd own a roomful of Fra Angelico paintings and another room would be chockablock with Botticelli. (Yes, I'd have the *Primavera* all to myself!) My dining room would be bursting with Sargent's work including *The Daughters of Edward Darley Boit.* My bedroom would be wall-to-wall with paintings by Matisse and Van Gogh. Propped up in bed I'd be reading books by Mary Ann Evans, known by her pen name as George Eliot. I'd reread her *The Mill on the Floss* while lounging on Matisse's vivid Moroccan fabric collection that he lovingly depicts in his paintings. I'd keep everything written by PG Wodehouse handy of course and, assuming that on my planet I'd live more or less forever (!), I'd play Bach for the first thousand years or so and then move on to Duke Ellington, Vivaldi, Miles Davis, Mozart, Beethoven and U2. Hendrix, the Stones and the

Jefferson Airplane would rattle my windows from time-to-time when I needed a break from Bach's B minor Mass. I'd listen to a lot of opera too including *La Cenerentola,* by Gioachino Rossini. I'd watch Fellini's movies and everything else by my favorite Italian directors from Pietro Germi's *Divorce Italian Style* to Paolo Sorrentino's *The Great Beauty...*

But that's just me. I'm pretty old fashioned in my tastes. Luckily art made in the near past (and the present too) has its fair share of genius. Dale Chihuly, an American abstract glass sculptor who makes exquisitely crafted works, has proved that abstraction combined with the highest level of traditional craft can produce stunning beauty. Chihuly has the burns on his arms and face to prove his (un-Hirst-like) hands-on expertise. Chihuly is a visionary artist and one of the greatest craftsmen of all time. He is a living rebuke to the conceptual nothingness promoted by much of the art establishment that seems so wary of expertise and dismisses the idea of beauty as mere sentimentality.

The graffiti artist Banksy is another great working artist as well as being an idealist. His unabashedly beautiful pieces of street art carry socially charged messages, while his visual sermons on social justice, for instance expressed on the wall imprisoning the Palestinian people or highlighting the plight of the poor, speak to me of his deep spiritual empathy. Some of Banksy's work also exhibits a level of hands-on representational craft that Leonardo would have appreciated.

John Cage composed his *4'-33"* of silence in 1952 as his Bloomsbury-like rebuke to tradition and to music itself. On 7 July, 1956, music found its defender at the Newport Jazz festival. This defense of the sublime left ordinary people speechless with joy until they found their voices and roared their approval and danced. Thunderstorms had hit the outdoor event. Fans were leaving. Then Duke Ellington asked his tenor saxophonist Paul Gonsalves to play Ellington's 1937 tune: "Diminuendo and Crescendo in Blue." Gonsalves played improvised choruses. The record producer George Avakian later wrote: "Halfway through Paul's solo, it had become an enormous, single, living organism." Leonard Feather, reviewing the show for *Down Beat* wrote: "Here and there in the reduced, but still multitudinous crowd, a couple got up and started jitterbugging. Within minutes, the whole of Freedom Park was transformed as if struck by a thunderbolt. Hundreds of spectators climbed up on their chairs to see the action; the band built the magnificent arrangement to its peak and the crowd, spent, sat limply wondering what could follow this."

Duke Ellington, America's greatest composer, was in tune with the hunger for beauty coded into the very fabric of human DNA. Evolution has a direction. Duke Ellington was one purpose-filled result. Scientific materialism and its metaphysical faith in ultimate meaninglessness were overthrown by Ellington that night in the same way that Renaissance artists and poets and Enlightenment philosophers overthrew the magical thinking of the medieval world. If evolution has no direction or purpose, what on earth was Duke Ellington doing here? If Duke Ellington isn't a good enough reason for the existence of the universe, what is?

Lightning also struck when the bestselling jazz record of all time (so far), Miles Davis's *Kind of Blue*, was recorded. *Kind of Blue* featured seven musicians in their prime: tenor saxophonist John Coltrane, alto saxophonist Julian "Cannonball" Adderley, pianists Bill Evans and Wynton Kelly, bassist Paul Chambers, drummer Jimmy Cobb, and trumpeter Miles Davis. In the mid-1950s, Davis was inspired by the work of pianist Bill Evans. Evans was an essential contributor to the *Kind of Blue* recording because Evans introduced Davis to classical composers including Béla Bartók and Maurice Ravel. To me the result is up there with Bach's *Brandenburg Concertos* for the sublime wonder it pours into my soul. Many great rock musicians of the 1960s referred to *Kind of Blue* for inspiration. Pink Floyd keyboardist Richard Wright said that the album influenced the structure of the introductory chords to the song "Breathe" on one of the greatest rock albums of all time, *The Dark Side of the Moon.*

———

Photography has not broken the link between art, craft, spirituality and beauty either. This most technical art form allows some of its practitioners to make timeless works of beauty. Richard Avedon's *Marilyn Monroe* delves into the hollowness of our celebrity culture. Rembrandt would have appreciated the psychological depths of that timeless photograph. And Irving Penn (sometimes dismissed, like Avedon, as "just a fashion photographer") made great art during the 1940s and 1950s when some critics had falsely claimed that abstract expressionism had forever obliterated the relevance of representational expression.

For anyone who thinks that post-Duchamp, all art must forever be of the irony-saturated door-closing kind, I offer Penn's *Nude No. 57* as a rebuke to this deterministic view of art history. Penn's monumental photograph speaks to what we *are* independent of any training in art appreciation, evoking a sculpturally powerful fertility goddess. And it is timeless. Michelangelo found his truest heir in Penn. Michelangelo's *Night*—a female with flaccid belly and breasts as well as childbirth marks—paved the way for Penn's glorious female tributes.

My granddaughter Amanda and I went to see *Night* and *Day* in Florence when she was ten, a trip she still remembers fondly at twenty. We attended the Penn show together too. Years later she made the same connection between the works of Michelangelo and Penn and wrote this note to me in response to reading this chapter in manuscript form:

> I remember seeing Michelangelo's *Night* and *Day* with you! They were so beautiful and you told me about how they were unique in the way they showed the aging process. We were all in Italy together—Francis, Jessica, Ben, Grandma and you. There's a picture of us from this trip in your kitchen. I remember the trip being lovely but a bit stressed because you wanted to show us everything in a short amount of time!

Penn's exhibition at the Metropolitan Museum of Art entitled "Earthly Bodies: Irving Penn's Nudes, 1949–1950" was one of the greatest shows I've ever attended.

Stepping into the center of a room surrounded by Penn's velvety platinum prints, I watched Genie looking at his work. Genie stood with her hip thrust out, her arms folded, her figure curved in a relaxed S-shape, totally in keeping with Penn's pictures celebrating the female form. I was doubly smitten watching the woman I love gaze at Penn's lovingly rendered women.

And then there's my hero Diane Arbus!

Arbus's photographs explore her personal generosity and compassion much as Penn's photographs lovingly and respectfully explore the female form. Arbus is our very own American Pieter Breughel the Elder. In a working life of fewer than ten years, Arbus's pictures reached past our prejudice, homophobia and class consciousness just as Breughel memorialized peasants, beggars and the dispossessed (the least of these of his day) instead of kings and princes.

Amanda added this note in the margins of this chapter when she read an early draft:

> I remember learning about Arbus in art class [in her Finnish public high school] and especially looking at her photograph of *Boy with Grenades*. We were talking about portraying a 'different' kind of beauty than the traditional kind. Arbus often printed the oddest looking photo of a person, this is the case in the photo *Boy with Grenades*, the boy in this photo is actually completely normal looking otherwise, just not in this photo. While talking about Arbus we also talked about a Finnish photographer, Elina Brotherus, known for her odd self-portraits.

Arbus's subjects, like the eight-year-old boy staring happily into the camera *while* clutching two hand grenades, seem to know that she values them as much as Breughel's peasant models seem to also understand. Both artists recorded the lives of outsiders and outcasts. Both folded their subjects into the human family in an inclusive embrace. Both gave their subjects the respect of a perfected craft, hands-on work, and dedication.

Brilliant, humane and accessible artists like Thiebaud, Banksy, Ellington, Davis, Chihuly, Arbus and Penn, not to mention generations of other great artists, musicians and conductors, had their work cut out for them during and after the twentieth century. They labored during a period of art history when serious artists had to struggle to survive a concentrated toxic dose of willful meaninglessness.

Notwithstanding a century-long assault, our perception of beauty still seems to have universal elements. John Singer Sargent is deservedly back in fashion, notwithstanding the best efforts of a generation of art critics bent on retraining our brains according to a sliver of modernist philosophy, now (thankfully) itself displaced by a more tolerant post-modernism. Music too survived the modernist assault. Most people avoid post-Schoenberg atonal music, aside from a few experts who cling to a cerebral approach to art that reduces it to a philosophical statement.

The people have spoken. Duke Ellington rules as does Miles Davis. And rock is many things but it's not atonal.

With each album and concert, the Irish quartet U2 has made tonal craft-rich music of lasting substance that has enjoyed massive popular acclaim. Their work is meaning-saturated and produced hands-on as un-fooled-around-with straight up rock! It is rife with overt spiritual content. U2 have, at times, been the most popular band in the world and also, arguably, one of the most important musically. And they place a premium on high artistic craft as if the likes of Hirst and company never existed. U2's art is many things but never a prank. "We had no interest in being the biggest if we weren't the best," guitarist Dave "The Edge" Evans told *Rolling Stone* in 2004. "That's the only way being the biggest would mean anything."

U2's albums *War* (1983), *The Joshua Tree* (1987) and *All That You Can't Leave Behind* (2000) are classics. Bono's struggle for causes like Third World debt relief and U2's participation in rock-for-charity events including Live Aid and Amnesty International's "Conspiracy of Hope" tour have been motivated by an unashamedly religious humanistic non-ironic ethic. And U2's music opens doors for other bands to follow. They see themselves as servants of a great tradition, not smashers of the past. Instead of mocking their chosen art they have struggled to perfect it.

Like the best rock, rap and pop, film scores are also still stubbornly tonal as is country, rap, DJ-created techno-dance tracks, blues and jazz. Why hasn't atonal music caught on after more than a hundred years of earnest striving by dedicated composers and professional critics? These days the failure of certain forms of ideological modernism appears to have a scientific explanation. Humans share common aesthetic ideas that arise directly from our physical beings. Maybe this is because our brains process sound in an orderly manner so we can survive.

Neurobiologists and ethnomusicologists explore how melody, rhythm and harmony affect people. For example, after building up tension through modulation, repetition and contrast, most music eventually resolves to the tonic through a series of familiar chord progressions. Although cultural preferences and early ear training play a role—and the word *tonality* can sometimes be used in a way that has excluded non-Western music—basic musical preferences *transcend* specific cultures.

It turns out that taste in music is about more than bourgeois Western values being imposed. We humans are drawn to narratives through musical experiences, be those experiences in the context of classical music, jazz, rap or rock, characterized by conflict or tension followed by eventual resolution. In some ethnomusicologists' experiments Western classical music has been played for people who have never been exposed to our society. Nevertheless, when asked to identify what mood the music evoked they designated passages as "happy" or "sad" the same way a Western listener would.

—

The war on traditional notions of narrative, order and beauty has failed. Representational, story-driven movies are embraced by most people, rather than the installation and performance art favored by big galleries and institutions like Tate Modern. The Whitney Biennial (an exhibition of contemporary American art) is often dispiriting to all but a few critics, curators and art students. (Why do curators write longer and longer explanations of the art in their shows in direct proportion to less and less content, craft or expertise?) Badly made conceptual dreck, crafted by committee in a "process" is mostly just boring.

American television is in the midst of a golden age of classical, even Shakespearean story-driven, hands-on, writer-centric, tradition-connected creativity *despite* the best efforts of the now-irrelevant deconstructionist literary theorists of the 1960s and 1970s. Shows like *Breaking Bad* and *House of Cards* explore "old fashioned" pre-Bloomsbury classical themes of good and evil to wild global popular acclaim. Wasn't moral argument through theater supposed to have ended with the absurdist theater of Surrealism and Dadaism? Did Jean Genet, Jean Tardieu and Samuel Beckett strive in vain?

Most people seem to vote with their feet, ears and eyes for spirituality-laden aesthetic traditions that, like the Dude, abide. Video games are increasingly representational. Furthermore, the "rebellious young" are reviving representational art through their ubiquitous tattoos!

And what of the almost spiritual sense of mission that characterizes the entrepreneurs in Silicon Valley startups? Correctly viewing themselves as liberators, our science-based geeks have invented terms fraught with spiritual overtones. We now send our books, our music and even our memories into a cloud. We may or may not believe in God but we *do* once again believe in meaningful consciousness residing outside of ourselves.

Spirituality is overtaking commerce while commerce looks more and more like art—the kind of art the Medici or Irving Penn, Homer or Miles Davis would have understood in which artist and observer comprehend one another, even respect each other and speak a common language. More young people (and a few old ones like me) binge/stream made-for-TV programs like Netflix's traditionally crafted Shakespeare-inspired *House of Cards* or the brilliant Australian show (one of my favorites) *Rake*, than will visit the Tate Modern or Whitney in a year.

Maybe the future no longer belongs to the anti-meaning ideologues. Shakespeare is produced tens of thousands of times more often than the absurdist plays. Miles Davis lasted, Cage didn't. Duchamp's "original" urinal got lost and had to be replaced by one crafted by a ceramic artist. The museum wanted to keep their investment in a piece of art that was meant to mock the art market! The "found object" became the made investment. Hirst's reputation is rotting along with his sharks. Daniel Dennett has a following but even his followers behave *as if* their lives have a deeper meaning than plant life, no matter what he says to the contrary. And modern delivery systems are bypassing the critics and gatekeepers. Who needs another rotting shark in a tank of formaldehyde or a hank of cloth hung from the Whitney's ceiling as a "statement" of something or other when you can watch *QI* (*Quite Interesting*) the wonderful British comedy quiz show on YouTube for free? It's hosted by Stephen Fry, a greatly talented defender of good writing and music. (Who would have guessed his musical hero is Wagner?)

A new generation is embracing human connection rather than debunking it. The liberating results are real. The geeks (bless them) are killing off the jaded cold hearted gatekeepers. When I was a young artist in the 1970s I had to travel to a gallery, slides in sweaty hand, and beg for a meeting with the owner if I wanted to sell a painting. If the owner loved my work, I'd be invited back and a year or two later he or she would put a few paintings in a show. (I wandered off into the movie business and quit painting.) When I resumed painting in 2006, I worked for eight years until I liked my work enough to show it. I started a website in 2014 and now sell art directly to collectors. There are no gatekeepers in sight. It's just me directly in touch with people who like my work.

The same goes for my writing. I self-published this book. Given the bestselling status of some of my previous books, several of my former secular publishers and several religious publishers were interested in publishing it. However they wanted me to craft this book to fit their marketing strategies. "Does it go on the New Atheist or the Religion shelf?" they asked. "Can you rewrite it to fit one or the other market?"

My answer was no. Yet you are reading the book I wrote.

I don't view you as a market segment. I view you as my partner, an individual reader, a friend as complex and maybe even as conflicted, as I am. Why should either of us "fit" anywhere?

My liberators in Silicon Valley have freed me to write for you directly and to say what I want to say to anyone I want to say it to. The Internet and its innovators are doing more to facilitate the reemergence of content-laden, craft-rich, hands-on art, individuality and perhaps even spirituality, than all the galleries, agents, critics, churches and publishers combined.

XXIV

When I first met Camilla Tilling she was headed to Boston to sing in Mahler's Symphony Number Four. This is traditionally described as "a musical journey from earth to heaven." The music she was about to sing struck me as crazily fitting. If anyone believed in heaven it was my mother. And if anyone *wanted* to believe in heaven, on the day after I'd stood next to her coffin, it was me.

Camilla was the star of the program and was to be led by the renowned conductor Bernard Haitink. So I was thrilled to receive this email from Camilla the day after we'd met.

> Re: Meeting on Swiss [the national airline]... Flying, is always about getting to your destination. Like a big gap of time that you forget when you get out of the plane. Yesterday was a big serendipity, thank you!!! There will be two tickets under your name in the box office for Tuesday. Maestro Haitink is amazing, I heard a bit of the rehearsal with the orchestra today and it gave me goose bumps.

Following the concert Genie and I joined Camilla for dinner with Haitink, his wife and the artistic directors of the Boston Symphony and the New York Philharmonic. (Mom never did anything by halves!) The entire experience just seemed too good to be true. It reminded me of those times when I was a young child and Mom and Dad departed for a speaking trip. I'd be lonely the first night they were away but always discovered that Mom had left me surprise gifts to be opened after she was gone—reminders of her love.

The gift of Camilla's solo from Mahler's symphony replayed in my mind as we drove home. Genie and I could not help but laugh. Mahler's lyrics—about a child's entrance into paradise no less—gave Mom the last word, *again*!

> *No worldly tumult*
> *is to be heard in heaven.*
> *All live in greatest peace.*
> *We lead angelic lives,*
> *yet have a merry time of it besides.*
> *We dance and we spring,*
> *We skip and we sing.*

———

Camilla, her husband and Genie and I became friends when they visited our home while they were on yet another concert tour. In our conversations we revisited our journeys away from the religions we were raised in. Camilla and I discovered that we both still found meaning in our religious upbringings.

But what had we journeyed *to*? As to that I can only speak for myself.

———

Just as I find myself in two or more states of mind about so many things, I also find everything I experience multifaceted. Everything is unspeakably wonderful *and* unspeakably awful.

The universe is random and violent. That random violence is unbearably beautiful and seems to speak of purpose. That contradictory pattern also holds true when it comes to my personal experience of what it means to be human.

Juxtapose these words, and the stunningly beautiful music that brings them to life...

> *No worldly tumult*
> *is to be heard in heaven.*
> *All live in greatest peace.*

... with this excerpt from *Night,* a book by Elie Wiesel about his experience in the German concentration camps.

> One day, as we returned from work, we saw three gallows... The SS [guards] seemed more preoccupied, more worried, than usual. To hang a child in front of thousands of onlookers was not a small matter. The head of the camp read the verdict. All eyes were on the child. He was pale, almost calm, but he was biting his lips as he stood in the shadow of the gallows... "Where is merciful God, where is He?" someone behind me was asking. At the signal, the three chairs were tipped over... Then came the march past the victims. The two men were no longer alive... The child, too light, was still breathing... And so he remained for more than half an hour, lingering between life and death... Behind me, I heard the same man asking: "For God's sake, where is God?" And from within me, I heard a voice answer; "Where is He? This is where—hanging here from this gallows..."

Where is God when a gunman shoots children in a school, when Holly Meade dies in the midst of meeting a grandson, or when a child is hanged in Auschwitz? Either God is evil and should be punched in the mouth, or there is no God.

Which is it?

Perhaps there is another possibility: Jesus' co-suffering love is the best lens through which to reconsider God, or at least to reconsider ourselves.

———

I can blather on about art forever but the shadow cast by a hanged child obliterates my view of creation. The God of the Bible is of little help since—if you favor a literal interpretation of the bible—that God is apparently a vindictive monster, trapped in one of the most inconsistent and corrosive books ever compiled.

In the Bible's God rages at his chosen people for *not* following his demands to kill every man, woman and child. The SS guards who hanged a child would be right at home in the ancient Israelite army murdering the Canaanites for land. Even some sayings attributed to Jesus make him out to be delusional, mean and trapped in pre-Enlightenment ignorance. René Girard can wish that there were a consistent redemptive thread running through the entire Bible. Dream on!

As a raised-to-believe Christian, like Girard, I too hope that the nicer parts of the Bible represent a truer version of the Creator than the rest of this insufferably inconsistent collection of texts. That's hardly enough to cling to.

———

Those of us raised in the Christian tradition need to choose to either see God in Jesus or to continue to let the Bible define God. Our tradition says that Jesus is God. Maybe we should act as if we think he is instead of worshipping a book. Maybe we should be brave enough to admit that we are compelled to either become blinded ideologues or we need to forthrightly pick and choose *what* we follow in the Bible. Most Christians do that anyway, many just don't admit it.

Unbelievers relying on generic human goodness for hope of a better future are hardly off the hook either. The problem is always *how* to define goodness. People like my friend Sam look to science for answers, or to what the *New York Times* says, or to whatever else they are "into" at any given moment. That is preferable to exclusively looking to the Bible for solutions but it hardly answers the question: How do we define goodness and who can set us an example of what goodness looks like in action?

Given my background these questions make me think about Jesus. But Jesus is far away and long ago and the book about him is a mess. So I look for closer-to-home examples of people who have tried to follow Jesus according to the most enlightened interpretations of who and what he was. And that brings me to Mother Maria.

XXV

"Mother Maria of Paris is a saint of our day and for our day; a woman of flesh and blood possessed by the love of God." So wrote British intellectual and Orthodox bishop Harold Bloom. Born to a prominent Russian Orthodox family, Mother Maria (then Elizaveta Pilenko) renounced her religious beliefs at age fourteen when her father died. She later became a committed atheist and Bolshevik. In 1910 she married and was drawn to both literary and leftist revolutionary circles, divorcing in 1913. The anti-communist White Army took control of her town and tried her as a communist, but the judge was a former teacher of hers and Mother Maria was acquitted. The two fell in love, had an affair and eventually married.

Mother Maria and her husband fled Soviet Russia, arriving in Paris in 1923. By then she was studying theology and doing social work among impoverished Russian exiles. After her second marriage dissolved, she had an illegitimate child. Mother Maria began her journey back to Christianity, explaining, "Christ also died. He sweated blood. They struck his face." But her faith was messy. She didn't have the outward appearance of holiness and she was the sort of person good people avoided. In Paris her Orthodox bishop—aware of her work on behalf of the poor and also keenly aware of her failed marriages—encouraged Mother

Maria to take vows, which she did only with his promise that she would not have to live in a convent. So she became a nun because of a bishop who allowed her to dictate terms.

Scandal!

In 1932, Mother Maria took the monastic Christian name Maria and turned her rented house in Paris into a hybrid commune/homeless shelter/intellectual/theological salon/food pantry/bar rolled into one. She drank! She chain smoked! She ate meat during Lent! She never denounced or converted the debauched intellectuals and artists of Paris who were her friends!

As Jerry Ryan wrote in a review of *Mother Maria Skobtsova: Essential Writings,* "Many were scandalized by Mother Maria. This woman had been twice divorced, had an illegitimate child by another man, had leftist political sympathies and was an eccentric. At her becoming a nun she took the name of Maria in memory of St. Mary of Egypt, a prostitute who became an extreme crazed ascetic."

As Ryan notes, Mother Maria continued to scandalize. Her clothes were filthy with grease from the kitchen and paint from her workshop. She stank. She frequented bars, had no patience with long Orthodox liturgies, and found strict ascetic fasts impossible to keep. Any self-respecting bishop would have kicked her out. She was the wrong kind of nun. As Olivier Clement writes in the preface to Ryan's book.

> If we love and venerate Mother Maria it is not in spite of her disorder, her strange views and her passion. It is precisely these qualities that make her so extraordinarily alive among so many bland and pious saints. Unattractive and dirty, strong, thick and sturdy, yes, she was truly alive in her suffering, her compassion, her passion.

Mother Maria dismissed people like me who were preoccupied with their spiritual lives and so-called personal relationships with God. She would probably have dismissed most of this book as self-indulgent. According to her, my sort of spiritual narcissism must be abandoned if one hopes to truly love as Jesus loved. Mother Maria wrote:

> In our time Christ and the life-giving Holy Spirit demand the whole person. The only difference from state mobilization is that the state enforces mobilization [to care for people], while our faith waits for volunteers. And, in my view, the destiny of mankind depends on whether these volunteers exist and, if they do, how great their energy is, how ready they are for sacrifice.

Mother Maria said that Christian egocentrism is a contradiction in terms. In her essay "Types of Religious Life," she denounced the Orthodox Church's institutional structures, rituals, even aesthetic beauty, as dead ends. She also dismissed "trends of social Christianity... based on a certain rationalistic humanism [that] apply only the principles of Christian morality to 'this world' and do not seek a spiritual and mystical basis for their constructions."

———

After the fall of France to the Germans and after the collaborationist Vichy government required Jews to wear the yellow star, Mother Maria wrote this poem entitled "Israel."

> *Two triangles, a star,*
> *The shield of King David, our forefather.*
> *This is election, not offense.*
> *The great path and not an evil.*

Once more in a term fulfilled,
Once more roars the trumpet of the end;
And the fate of a great people
Once more is by the prophet proclaimed.
Thou art persecuted again, O Israel,
But what can human malice mean to thee,
who have heard the thunder from Sinai?

Jews came to Mother Maria begging for Christian baptismal certificates in order to escape deportation. To help them was to risk death, but Mother Maria took in Jews and gave them forged documents declaring them non-Jews. Her house was soon bursting at the seams. Mother Maria once remarked, "It is amazing that the Germans haven't pounced on us yet." If anyone came looking for Jews, she said, she would show them an icon of the Mother of God.

A children's book I read to Lucy, *Silent as a Stone, St. Maria of Paris and the Trash Can Rescue*, tells the story of Mother Maria saving Jewish children. Her home was near the cycling stadium of Vélodrome d'Hiver, where the Jews were held on their way to deportation. The book is based on firsthand accounts of what Mother Maria accomplished during her visits to that stadium in June of 1942. As those who had been rounded up awaited deportation to the camps, Mother Maria used her status as a nun to bring food to the families waiting for transport. Then she smuggled some of their children out of the stadium in trashcans under the guise of helping with sanitation. The hygienic Germans allowed this, never suspecting that each trash can had a small terrified child huddled inside. Those children often became the only survivors in their families.

Mother Maria risked everything for the very people who in Russia had often been persecuted by anti-Semitic Orthodox. Then, on February 8, 1943 the Germans arrested Mother Maria, her son, Yuri, her priest, Father Dmitri, and their helper, Elia Fondaminski.

Father Dmitri was interrogated by Hans Hoffman, a Gestapo officer. A portion of the interrogation has been preserved, as transcribed by the ever meticulous Nazis.

> **Hoffman:** "If we release you, will you give your word never again to aid Jews?"
>
> **Father Dimitri:** "I can do no such thing. I am a Christian and must act as I must."
>
> **Hoffman:** (striking the priest across the face.): "Jew lover! How dare you talk of helping those swine as being a Christian duty?"
>
> **Father Dimitri:** (holds up the crucifix from his cassock): "Do you know this Jew?"

Mother Maria was sent to the Ravensbrück concentration camp. Prisoners who survived have shared some of their memories: "She exercised an enormous influence on us all," wrote one survivor after the war. "No matter what our nationality, age, political convictions—this had no significance whatever. Mother Maria was adored by all. The younger prisoners gained particularly from her concern. She took us under her wing. We were cut off from our families, and somehow she provided us with a family."

One account of Mother Maria's martyrdom says that on Easter Saturday, 1945, she took the place of a woman who was about to be sent to the gas chamber. Another account has Mother Maria going to the gas chamber without taking someone's place. Either way, she was killed *only* because she chose to save others by imitating Jesus, even unto death.

Mother Maria saved those that many in her own church had killed in countless Church-approved pogroms. To me, Mother Maria's death is an example of love embraced as a stark life-changing and essential *fact* as real as the carbon compounds that form the basis of life.

XXVI

I say the Nicene Creed. I say the words "I believe" this and that. I say these words in good conscience, because saying I believe in God is not the same as saying I *know* what those words mean. I don't. Words fall short. I don't know what words such as "Light of Light, very God of very God, begotten, not made, being of one substance with the Father" mean. Then again I don't know what the words "I love you, Genie" mean either. I say those words with all sincerity, too, but also in blind ignorance of their ultimate meaning.

Rational argument is not the point. I know I love Genie because I find myself cleaning the house in anticipation of her return from a trip. I find myself putting flowers in her office and in the kitchen. I do these things without thinking. These actions are as close to proof of love as I'll get.

The actions are not an argument but evidence of a love that seeks to make the daily life of one woman as blissful as possible. Neuropsychology and religion are not the point. The point is that Genie walks into a clean house, and there are flowers. And that is in spite of the fact I have sometimes treated her horribly.

I say the words "I love you." I know I mean them though because I take half a day to clean, to shop for flowers, to think about taking Genie to bed, to experience a flutter of anticipation as she walks out of the airport concourse and I see her again. Yet while waiting for her there I've been casually watching a flight attendant's ass. I've been a saint and sinner, a jerk and a better man than I once was, loved by my wife, children and grandchildren, yet sometimes still a tyrant.

The words of the Creed and my words of love are metaphors for something that is ultimately indescribable but ever present and never perfect. What I *know* is that *whatever* the Creed means, I have been overwhelmed by love. I have seen "Light of Light" in action, *felt* its power while not understanding from whence the light pours into me.

———

I was shuffling forward in the communion line, with Lucy in my arms. I was lost in gloomy thoughts, brooding on my past and on my doubts, my failures, and my meanness to Genie when I was young, stupid and so woefully controlling. I was feeling that going to church was a waste of time. I was feeling unworthy in every sense of the word and sinking into a gray depression.

Lucy and Jack are always in and out of my arms in church as they have been since they were born. So I'd actually forgotten I was holding her. (These days I hardly know how to be in church without a grandchild riding on my hip.) With my head bowed and my eyes closed I shuffled forward to the chalice to receive the "body and blood" through a ritual I don't comprehend and that seemed entirely pointless that day. I was adrift in my melancholy. Then I felt the touch of Lucy's hand on my face and—startled—opened my eyes.

It took me a moment to remember where I was. Lucy was gazing into my face. She wasn't smiling, just gazing at me in that straightforward way that only a child achieves: with serious concentration and offering me a transparent "look" that had no agenda. She wanted nothing from me. All I saw in Lucy's expression was unconditional trust. All I saw was a child who knows me *now* and who never expects anything but kindness from me. She did not know of my past sins, failings and bitter self-accusing regrets. Lucy was not judging me. I was accusing myself while she was just gently touching her Ba's cheek, checking to see why my eyes were closed.

Lucy inclined her head and kissed me. This thought crashed into my brain: I am being seen *as I'd like to be perceived*, not as I see myself. I have seen the face of God.

———

I do not always believe let alone know if God exists. I do not always know he, she or it does not exist either, though there are long patches in my life when it seems God never did exist. What I *know* is that I see the Creator in Jesus or nowhere. What I *know* is that I see Jesus in my children and grandchildren's love. What I *know* is that I rediscover *hope* again and again through Genie's love. What I *know* is that Mother Maria *loved* unto death. What I know is that sometimes something too good to be true, is true.

I have seen Genie forgive me. She has been my co-sufferer rather than my judge. My heart beats faster when we're making love and I look into Genie's face that's ever young to me, even as the calendar tells me that my wife is sixty-two. How can both facts be true? What does the *actual* historical Genie Schaeffer *really* look like at any one point?

The way I see Genie is as true as any scientific measurements a dermatologist might take while preparing to do fractional resurfacing to lessen the effects of sun damage. Both truths—the dermatologist's and mine —are equally genuine. Both ways of seeing are valid, even empirically true, notwithstanding they contradict each other. Genie is *actually* ever young to me. She's also *actually* sixty-two. The dermatologist has his science to prove a point about the condition of Genie's skin. I have the truth of a forty-four-year love affair to offer her as an equally valid fact. That truth is "only in my head." So is everything else.

———

My fear of meaninglessness comes from one place: my own willfully closing my eyes to the mystery of wonder. This is the same mistake I make when I look to physical remedies to stop the aging process or to words about love rather than to loving *actions.* If Genie were fixated on the literal aging process, she'd be more in the grip of aging than ever, not less. The truest mirror of my wife's youthfulness is found in my eyes, not in a dermatologist's scalpel or injection. Our fear of meaninglessness comes from allowing ourselves to be forced to make a choice, as it were, between the science of what Genie looks like and the truth of how she looks to her lover. When we lose hope, we're seeing everything, so to speak, from the dermatologist's point of view and not through the lens of love.

Christ's love unto death and resurrection—however we interpret those words—is a means of freeing us from the anguish of mortality. Our desire for some sort of guarantee of eternal life and all fundamentalist attempts to describe it are self-defeating. Trying to nail down theological certainties is putting faith in our imagination rather than in God's. It is like me demanding an explanation from Lucy in that communion line as to *how* her love for me *works* rather than just holding her a little closer. Or put it this way: The clean kitchen Genie walked into and the flowers on her desk didn't need a card to explain them anymore than great art needs a curator's wall notice to make it intelligible.

Our best hope is not found in correct theology, the Bible or any other book, but in the love we express through action rather than words. Our best hope is that love predates creation and thus that the Creator sees us as ever young. Our hope is that when we look at God through the eyes of the loving Christ we will see who God really is. Our ultimate hope is that God will be looking back at us *as we'd like to be seen.*

Scientists have found direct evidence of the expansion of the universe, a previously theoretical event that took place a fraction of a second after the Big Bang nearly 14 billion years ago. The clue is encoded in the primordial cosmic microwave background radiation that continues to spread. My hope is that a trillionth of a second before the Big Bang, the energy animating the mystery of matter being created out of nothing was love.

XXVII

Five months after Holly died, one of her woodcuts was left at our back door. Genie was in California visiting her family so I was alone when I found it. There was no note or indication of how it got there. It wasn't wrapped, just sitting between the storm door and the main door.

The print is of two lovers clinging to each other while flying over a village. The work is reminiscent of Chagall's flying brides and grooms. The title, "I Am My Beloved's and My Beloved Is Mine," is from the Song of Solomon. It was written below the print in Holly's handwriting.

I picked up the woodcut. "Hi Holly," I said, tears filling my eyes.

I had never seen this print. Had Holly made it for me? Had she visited me?

When Genie came home a week later I learned that Holly's daughter had contributed the print to a fundraising art fair Genie was helping to organize at our church. This was the mundane explanation of *how* the print got to me. But how it got there was only one kind of truth. *Why* it was sitting at my back door was an entirely different matter.

I bought the print at the art fair, though I knew it already belonged to me. The print is propped up in front of me as I write this. It will stay there forever or until my body betrays me as Holly's betrayed her. Then—who knows—maybe Genie, my daughter Jessica, my sons Francis and John, my son-in-law Dani, my daughter-in-law Becky or my grandchildren Amanda, Ben, Lucy, Jack and Nora Rose—born to Becky and John the day I was doing the final copy edit of this book—will find the picture and believe that it's a message of eternal love from me.

And whatever the mundane circumstance of their finding it, they'll be right.

Acknowledgments

There would be nothing worth writing about without the love of my wife Genie, my daughter Jessica, my sons Francis and John, my son-in-law Dani, my daughter-in-law Becky and my grandchildren Amanda, Benjamin, Lucy and Jack. Thank you Genie for reading this book twice, making notes and supporting this project as you have supported so many others and for letting me invade your privacy—again!—for my art's sake. Thank you to Karen Wright Marsh for doing a careful edit of this book. Thanks to my son Francis for checking the manuscript and his excellent suggestions and detailed notes. Thank you to my granddaughter Amanda for your lovely notes. Thank you to Holly Hendricks for making my ideas flow more smoothly and for your very good editing and advice. Thanks to Kevin Miller for a great edit on an early draft. Thank you to Brad Jersak for dropping everything to read the book and for giving me excellent notes and then rechecking several new additions to the text. Thanks to my daughter-in-law Becky for her timely corrections. Thank you to my son John for a careful reading of the manuscript and timely corrections. (Thank you to Nora Rose for getting born just in time to make it into the last chapter!) Thank you Emily O'Brien for editing certain sections used here so well. Thanks to Fontaine Dollas Dubus for her careful read and for her notes. Thank you Paul Hawley for a careful read of the book and your timely copy edit.

Thanks to Elizabeth and Zack Keefe for their helpful comments. Sarah Johnson took the time to read the book, make notes and email me helpful suggestions. Thanks to Samir Selmanović for his friendship to this project and his good advice over the years I've been working on it. Thank you to Fr. Antony of St. Mary's Orthodox Church in Cambridge, MA, for his notes and advice. Thanks to Dan Russell for providing encouragement, friendship and inspiration to this project. Thanks to Vanessa Ayersman for reading the book and for making helpful notes. Thanks to Hal Fickett for his hard work on my social media sites that have put me in touch with so many readers who in turn asked the questions that I've tried to address here. And thanks to those readers who so kindly have emailed me and contacted me on Facebook and who read my work and respond. My readers make me feel as if I'm not wasting my time. Keep writing to me please! Lastly, thanks to the Create Space/Amazon team for making this so easy and to Amazon, YouTube, Twitter, Google and Facebook for opening so many doors.

Follow Frank on Twitter: www.twitter.com/frank_schaeffer

See Frank's paintings http://www.frankschaefferart.com/

Follow Frank on Facebook https://www.facebook.com/frank.schaeffer.16

Media contact Frank at frankaschaeffer@aol.com

ALL BOOK CLUBS WELCOME! I'll gladly do a Skype or phone session with you.